W9-BLK-399

FELT BOARD FUN

by
Liz & Dick Wilmes
art
Donna Dane

A BUILDING BLOCKS Publication
3893 Brindlewood, Elgin, Illinois 60120

© 1984 by Liz and Dick Wilmes

ISBN 0-943452-02-3
Library of Congress Catalog No. 84-071958

All rights reserved. No part of this publication may be
reproduced, stored in a retrieval system, or transmitted, in any
form, or by any means, electronic, mechanical, photocopying
or otherwise except for the inclusion of brief quotations in a
review or duplication of patterns by the purchasers for the
purpose of making felt board pieces. Multiple reproductions of
patterns or other sections of the book without the prior written
permission of the publishers is prohibited. Printed in the
United States of America.

COVER DESIGN: Pat and Greg Samata
               Samata Associates, Inc. Dundee, Illinois

GRAPHIC ASSISTANT: Jennifer Dobbin

PUBLISHED BY:
  BUILDING BLOCKS
  P.O. Box 31
  Dundee, Illinois 60118

DISTRIBUTED BY:
  GRYPHON HOUSE, Inc.
  P.O. Box 275
  Mt. Rainier, Maryland 20712

ISBN 0-943452-02-3

DEDICATED TO . . .

. . . the caring adults who help children grow and learn

Contents

Introduction

Using Felt Board Fun

FELT BOARD FUN has been written and illustrated to help you make your felt board an indispensable part of your classroom. Enjoy each activity with your group and then have the pieces available in one of the learning centers for individual and small group work. Rotate the pieces as you introduce new concepts and celebrate holidays.

Each unit begins by describing a variety of activities. Alongside each activity is a MAKE column. This is a list of the felt board pieces that you will need to make before doing the activity with the children. Patterns for each of these pieces are clearly marked and illustrated on the pages following the text in each unit. Some of the activities also have a PROP column. Items in this list are objects that you will need to gather to do the specific activity.

A unique feature of many of the patterns is that they are recognizable as silhouettes. This enables you to quickly and easily create the pieces you need just by using the heavy outline of each pattern. There is, however, enough detail in each pattern so that you can create your pieces to fill the needs of your group and the purposes for which you are doing the activity.

Most of the activities in FELT BOARD FUN use pieces which are identified, sequenced, matched, categorized, and so on. Some of the activities, however, use pieces in a different way. One type of activity is the "layered" activity, in which you have one piece, such as a child, and other pieces, such as clothes, which are laid on top of the main piece. Another type of activity is the "add-on" activity, in which the pieces attach to each other to form the completed figure. The felt puzzle is a good example of this type of activity. These activities have been illustrated with dotted lines to show you where to cut.

The patterns in this book have been illustrated to be used with groups of approximately ten or less children and displayed on a medium size felt board. If, however, your group size is greater and/or you have a larger felt board, you may want to make the patterns bigger to meet your specific needs. Here are two simple ways which will work well.

1. Using an overhead projector, enlarge the patterns to the size you need them. If your school does not have an overhead projector, call your public library and ask if you may borrow theirs. Inexpensive projectors are also available from many catalog companies.
2. Make a larger pattern for yourself by following the outline of the illustrated pattern approximately a half inch or more away from the initial illustration. This will create acceptable silhouettes for most patterns. On "people" patterns you will need to adapt the width and length of the neck to fit the rest of the body.

A complete index has been provided to help you locate any specific pattern you need. In addition to locating specific patterns, you can use the index to find patterns to create new units. For example:

CIRCUS: Clown, man on stilts, dog, elephant, lion, tiger, ball, seal, horse, bear, whistle, balloon man

TRANSPORTATION: Boat, train, car, bus, airplane, rocketship, big wheel

INSECTS: Ant, butterfly, ladybug, ant hill, flowers

THE SKY: Sun, stars, clouds, airplane, kite, hot air balloon, birds, butterflies

Make Your Felt Board Pieces

Pieces for your felt boards can be made in a variety of ways. Choose the best one for the activity you are doing.

1. When using felt, you must first transfer the pattern onto the fabric. You can do this several ways:

**Duplicate the pattern from the book. Cut it out. Outline the pattern onto the felt.

**If you do not have access to a duplicating machine, trace the pattern from the book onto a sheet of tissue paper, cut it out, and then make your felt pieces from the tissue pattern.

**Use a tracing wheel and dressmaker's carbon. Lay the felt and carbon paper under the pattern in the book. Using the tracing wheel, trace the pattern onto the different colors of felt you've chosen.

Glue the smaller pieces onto the main silhouette with fabric glue or slightly watered down white glue. If you want additional features on your felt pieces, use permanent, non-toxic markers.

It is best to use pieces made from felt when you are doing activities in which you will be layering pieces on top of each other. Felt adheres to felt better than pellon to pellon. By using all felt pieces, you will avoid the problem of the pieces falling off of your board.

If you keep your pieces flat by periodically ironing them, they will more easily stick to your felt board. Simply put all of your wrinkled pieces on the ironing board. Cover them with a thin cloth. Using the steam setting on your iron, press all of the pieces at one time.

2. Lay heavyweight pellon on top of the patterns. Because you can see through pellon, you can trace the pattern right onto the fabric. Color the pattern with embroidery ink, permanent, non-toxic markers or crayons. Once colored, cut out the piece.

Pellon is a good fabric from which to make felt board pieces, because it is quick and easy to use. It is ideal to use when the activity does not involve layering.

3. Duplicate the pattern. Color it. Cut it out and back it with a piece of felt.

Make Your Felt Boards

There are many sizes and styles of felt boards, some you can purchase and others you will want to make.

BASIC BOARDS: Get a heavy piece of cardboard or thin plywood. Wrap a piece of felt around it and tape the fabric to the back of the board. Construct this type of felt board in various sizes — lap board about 1 foot square for individual work; a medium size board about 1½ feet by 2 feet for small group work; and a large board for full group activities.

FOUR-IN-ONE-BOARD: Get a large, sturdy cardboard box from the grocery store. Tape the top and bottom closed. Cover the four remaining sides of the box with felt. Great for several children to use in the language center.

PORTABLE FELT BOARD: Using the instructions for the Basic Board, make a felt board approximately 12″ by 14″. Staple a loop of cord to the top of the board, so you can wear it around your neck. Choose a felt activity which correlates to the unit you are teaching. As you are talking with the children during free play, have individuals do the felt board activity. This works well for one to one teaching while supervising free play activities.

FELT FOLDERS: Cut a piece of posterboard 11″ by 17″. Fold it in half (11″ by 8½″). Reinforce the fold with a piece of duct tape. Fold it again to get a good crease. Open the posterboard and cover it with a piece of felt as described above. With this type of board leave a little slack in the felt so that it will close when completed.

Lay the felt pieces you want the children to use on one side of the board, close it, and put the felt board in a pocket folder. On the front of the folder draw a very simple picture to indicate what felt board activity is in the folder. For example, you might draw a square to indicate a shape activity. Put several felt folders on the manipulative shelf. The children can use them during free play.

BASIC CONCEPTS

MY BODY

Make

Photos backed with felt

Props

Take each child's photograph the first day of school

Tell us your name: Put all of the photographs of the children on the felt board. Point to one of the photos and say, *"Look at this photo carefully. If it is you stand up, tell us your name, and then tap your head."* As the child is tapping, talk with the others about the body parts s/he is using to tap his/her head. Then have everyone tap his/her own head. Point to another photo and say, *"Whoever's photo this is stand up, tell us your name, and jump up and down.'* Once again talk with the children about the body parts that the child is using. Have everyone stand up and jump for a few seconds. Continue until everyone has been able to identify him/herself and do an activity.

Make

Sets of hand and foot prints which could belong to different size people — man, small child, baby, woman, giant, etc.

Hand and foot prints: Put the pairs of hand and foot prints on the felt board. Point to each one and talk about whose hands and feet they might be. Then have the children cover their eyes. Mix up all of the pairs so none of them match. Challenge the children to 'pair up' the prints with their original mate.

When all of the prints are matched, talk about which set of hands and feet would belong to the same person. Put those sets together. Then say, *"Look at all of the hand and foot prints. Who sees a set that might belong to a baby?"* (Have a child come up and give you that set.) *"Who sees a set that could belong to a four year old?"* Have a child come up, take it off of the board, and give it to you. Continue until all of the hand and foot print sets are off of the board.

Make

Blank head
Variety of facial parts which fit the face:
    Pair of eyes
    Pair of eyebrows
    Nose
    Mouth
    Mustache
    Beard
Pair of ears
Chin
Hair

What's on a head: Put the blank head in the middle of the board. Put the features off to the sides. Look at the head. Talk about what things belong on a head. As you identify the different features, have the children touch those parts on their own heads.

Then put the appropriate features on the felt head. Identify each part as you add it to the character. Have the children look at the newly created character and guess who it might be — a mom, dad, baby, etc. Maybe the face really looks like someone they know.

Now that you have created the first character, let the children move around or change the parts and create another person. Once again guess who it might be. Do this several times, always identifying the pieces as you move them around.

After a variety of characters have been created, have different children bring you various features. For example, *"Lillian, bring me the eyes. Jon bring me the mustache."* Continue until you have all of the features. Then have the last child give you the head.

MY BODY

Make

Use a set of features
from the activity
WHAT'S ON A HEAD
Include:
    Pair of ears
    Nose
    Chin
    Mouth
    Pair of eyes
    Pair of eyebrows
    Blank head

What's on a face: Say the verse about the face.

WHAT'S ON A FACE

Here's a face,
Now let's begin.
It has two ears,
A nose and chin,
A mouth, two eyes,
With a bushy brow.
What's on a face?
We all know now!
        Dick Wilmes

Then put the face on the board. As you place the appropriate features on the face, have the children identify each. Then say the verse again. As you name each part, have a child come up and point to it on the felt face. Have the other children touch the facial part on themselves.

Repeat the verse, but this time do not say the feature, just point to it on the felt face. As you point, have the children call out the name.

Say the verse once more. This time take the feature off of the face as everyone says it.

Make

Boy
Girl

Winter
Boots
Snowmobile Suit
Scarf
Mittens
Hat

Spring
Raincoat and hat
Umbrella
Sweater
Rubber boots

Summer
Shorts
T-shirt
Gym shoes

Fall
Sweatshirt with hood
Jeans
Long sleeve turtle-
   neck shirt

Dress for the season: Have the boy or girl on the felt board and the clothes for the four seasons in front of you. Name a season, talk a little bit about the weather and what clothes would be appropriate for that season.

Then put the felt clothes for that season on the board. Dress the felt child in the appropriate clothes. As you do, talk about the body parts that the clothes are covering. You can also decide why the clothes are important for that season. Do this activity for each of the four seasons.

MY BODY

Make

Use the clothes
  from the activity
  DRESS FOR THE
  SEASON

Sort the clothes: Put a variety of clothes on the board. Say to the children, *"I'm looking for three pieces of clothes that fit on your feet."* Have a child come up and point to the three pieces of footwear. As the child points to them have the remaining children call out what they are. Continue by sorting the clothes as to which body parts they cover.

Make

Duplicate sets of 5
  felt children. The
  5 children should
  have different color
  hair, clothes, and
  features

Children mix-up: Have three, four, or five children come up to the front of the group and stand in a row so everyone can see them. Have the remaining children look at the order the children are standing in. Go down the row and say each person's name. Have the person tell the others what color hair and eyes s/he has and one other thing about his/her features such as if s/he has freckles, a pointed nose, etc. Then have the children, who are sitting down, close their eyes. Mix up the row of children. Now have the group uncover their eyes. Have one child rearrange the row back to its original order.

Once the children can play the game with real children, put one set of five felt children in a row on the board. Point to the first one and talk about him/her. Notice the color of his/her hair, clothes, size and other features. Go to the next one and discuss that child's features. Continue with all five children.

Cover up the first row of felt children with a piece of cardboard. Put the duplicate row of felt children on the board in random order. Let someone come up and put the second row of felt children in the same order as the first row. Uncover the first row and see if they match.

VARIATION: If your group of children is just beginning to learn memory and matching skills, do this activity while looking at the first set of felt children. Then progress to covering a set of three children and finally the entire set of five children.

Make

As detailed a felt
  person as your
  group is ready for

Puzzle person: Put the figure on the felt board. Identify as many parts as you can. As you identify each part on the felt figure, let the children find the same part on themselves.

Then cut the felt figure into six pieces (2 legs, 2 arms, head, and torso). Put the pieces on the board. See if the children can identify body parts when they are separated. Have a child come up and begin to put the body together again by combining two pieces. Have him/her tell the others what body parts s/he is joining. Then have several more children each add a piece until the entire figure is back together again.

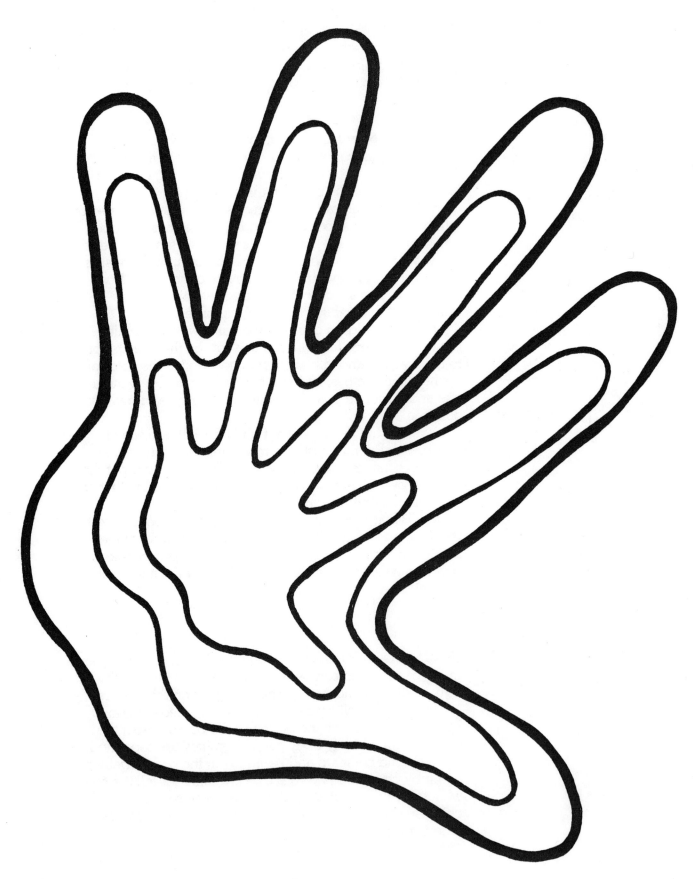

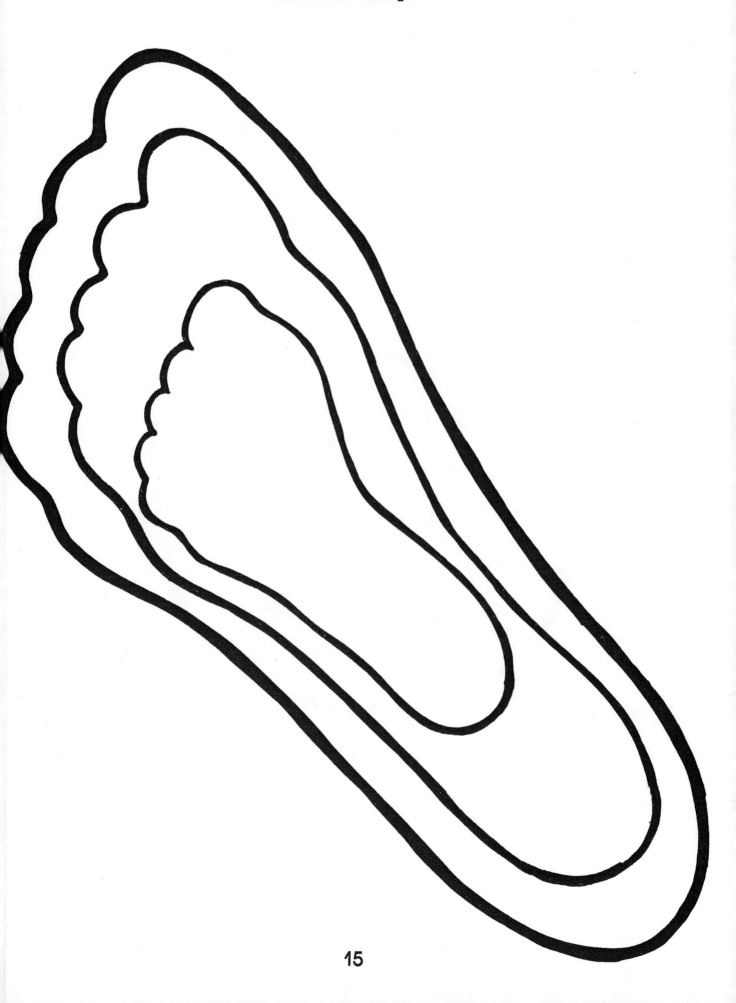

15

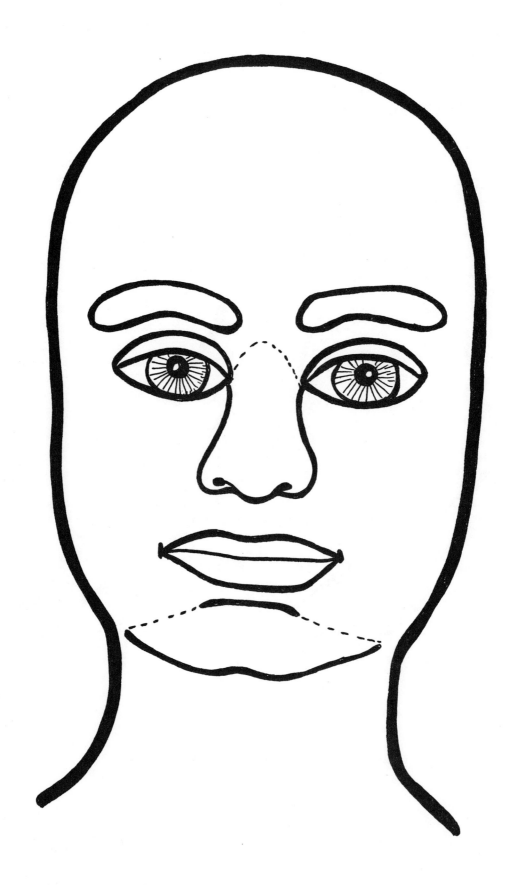

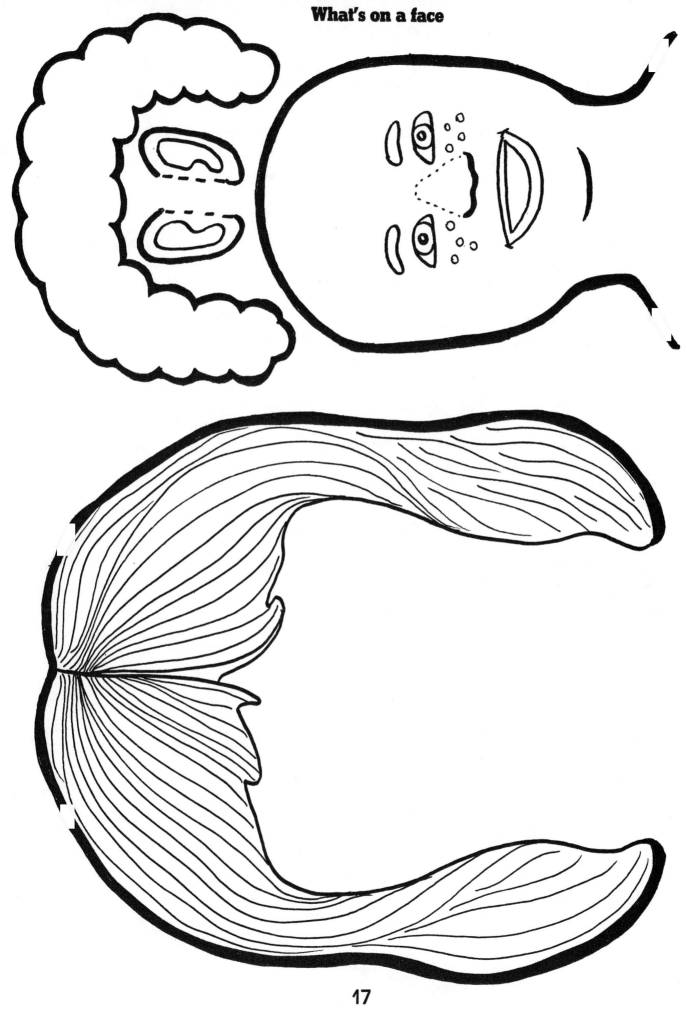

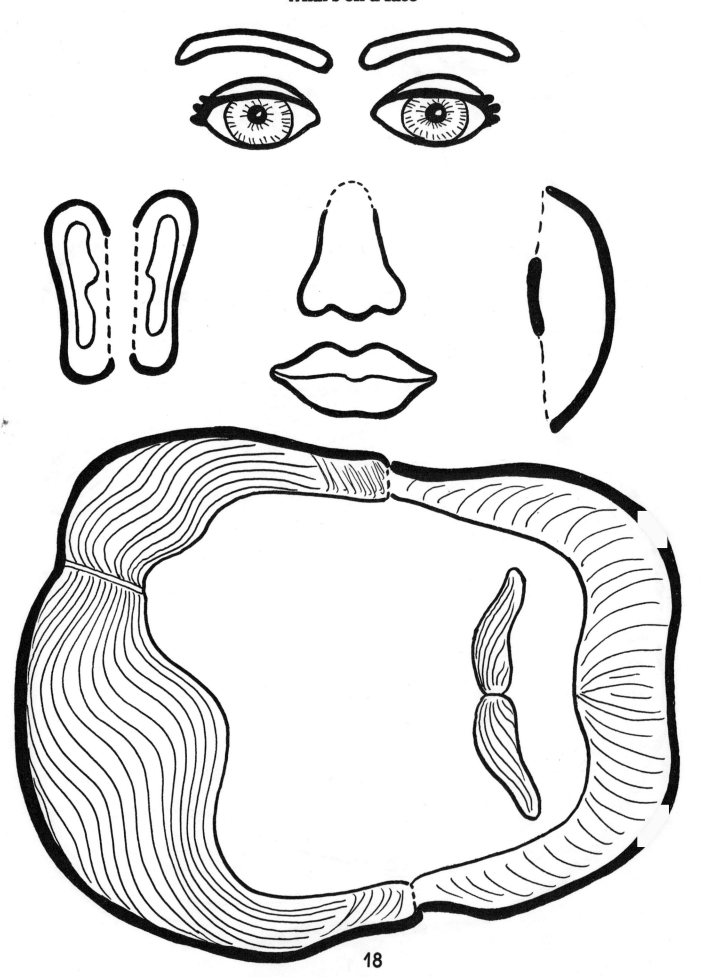

Dress for the season

Girl Pattern on Page 73

WINTER

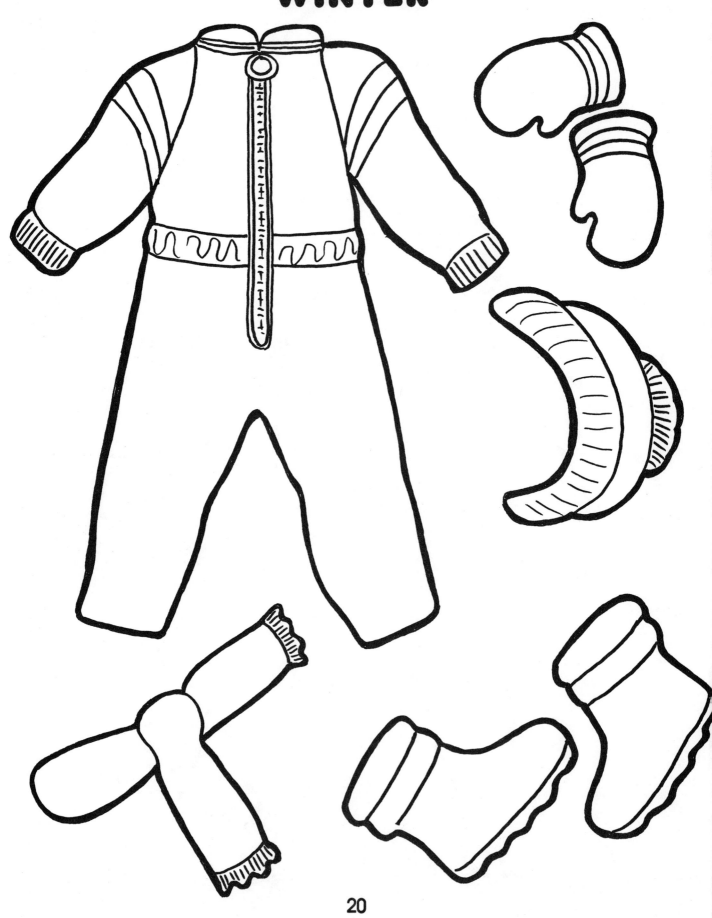

Dress for the season

SPRING

21

SUMMER

FALL

Make

Whistle
Clock
Ice cream cone
Apple
Fire in fireplace
Skunk
Man on stilts
Clown
Porcupine
Ice cube

Make

Drum
Maracas
Triangle
Cymbals
Tambourines
Rhythm sticks

Props

One of each type of
   rhythm instrument

Make

Angie
Jeannie
Kite
Cloud
Airplane
Concrete truck
Letter carrier
Dog
Bird
Cat
Tree
House
Mother

Using our senses: Put the felt pieces in front of you. Have the children name each of their senses and point to the body part which is mainly used for that sense. Put one of the felt pieces, for example the ice cream cone, on the felt board. Talk about which senses you use to experience an ice cream cone. (To extend this you could also discuss what senses you do not use to learn about the item.) Take the ice cream cone off of the board. Put another piece up. Once again decide which senses are most useful in learning about that item. Proceed in this manner until you have discussed all of the pieces. Conclude with this question, *"Were there any items for which you used all of your senses? Which one/s?"*

Listen carefully: Put all of the felt instruments on the board. Have the box of real rhythm instruments in front of you. Hold each one up, make its noise, and then have the children name it.

After they have used all of the rhythm instruments, have the children turn around and face away from the felt board. Choose one of the instruments, make its sound, and then hide it behind your back. Have the children turn back around and look at all of the felt pieces. Have the children figure out which one they heard. Take that felt piece off of the board and let one of the children hold it. Bring the real instrument out from behind your back. Does the real one match the felt piece? Continue the activity.

Coming home from school: Tell the children they are going to take a pretend walk with Angie and Jeannie. Put all of the felt pieces on the board. Point to each piece and have the children identify it. Then pass out the pieces to the children. Tell them that they will have to listen carefully, for you are going to need help as the story progresses. As you say the different things that the sisters see, the child holding the appropriate piece should put it on the board.

*"Angie and Jeannie are sisters. They live one block from their school. Everyday they walk to school and then home again. They enjoy their walk, for they always see many interesting things. One warm spring day, the first thing they saw when they left school was a **kite** flying high in the sky. As they were watching the kite, a **cloud** floated by. Way up in the sky they noticed a **plane** flying.* (Ask the children where the people in the airplane could be going.) *It was fun to look up at the sky, but a loud noise made them look across the street. A big **truck** had just begun pouring concrete for a new driveway at their friend's house. On they walked because they did not want to be late getting home. They passed the **letter carrier** and a man walking his **dog**. The dog barked "Hello" to Angie and Jeannie. They waved back. A **bird** flew into a newly budding **tree**. A **cat** saw the bird and ran up the tree after it, but the bird flew away.* (Ask the children what they think the cat did next.) *Angie and Jeannie saw their **house** so they began to run. When they got closer they saw their **mother** waiting for them.*

Make

Scarecrow face on a
    felt pole
Shirt
Boots
Pants
Gloves
Hat
Handkerchief
(Make each piece
    of clothing out
    of a different
    textured piece of
    fabric. Some fabrics
    will adhere to the
    felt board; others
    you'll need to
    back with a piece of
    felt.)

Dress the scarecrow: Put the scarecrow face on the board. Talk about why farmers and gardeners use them in their fields and how they are constructed. When people dress the scarecrows they use all types of old clothing. Usually these clothes do not match and are made from a variety of textures.

Now put the scarecrow's clothes on the board. Point to each piece and have the children identify it. Then take one piece of clothing, for example the shirt, off of the board. Pass it around so that the children can feel the texture. Once they have felt the scarecrow's shirt, have them feel their own clothes. Ask if anyone is wearing clothes which feel the same as the scarecrow's shirt. Let them tell the others and compare the textures. Put the shirt in the correct place on the scarecrow. Continue in this manner until the scarecrow is dressed.

Make

Popcorn popper
    with cord
Oil
Bag of popcorn
    seeds
Measuring cup
Bowl
Mound of popped
    corn
Salt

Let's make popcorn: You use all of your five senses when you enjoy popcorn. Before you make it with the children at snacktime, pretend to make it using felt board pieces.

Have the felt oil, seeds, measuring cup, popper and bowl in front of you. Tell the children that they are going to help you make pretend popcorn. *"First you'll have to get everything you need to make popcorn."* Have the children name the things they need. As they name the different items, put them on the board. When they have all of the items ready, proceed to make a bowl of pretend popcorn. Go carefully through every step of the process, talking about each of the five senses used and the necessary safety precautions to make popcorn. Have the children manipulate the felt pieces just as they would if they were making real popcorn. Those children who are not using the felt pieces, can pretend to be plugging in the cord, measuring and pouring oil, and so on right where they are sitting.
EXTENSION: For snack that day make popcorn with the children. Talk about the ingredients and all of the other items you need. As you make the popcorn, reinforce each of the five senses that the children are using.

Make

Mushrooms
Green Peppers
Sausage
Pepperoni
Onions
Black olives
Cheese strips
8" red circle
   for each child

Props

Cut out 9" circle
   of posterboard for
   each child. Cover
   each of them with
   beige felt
Have bowls of fresh
   ingredients to
   match the felt
   pieces.

Create a pizza: Have the bowls of real ingredients and a pizza dough in front of you. Hold up one of the fresh ingredients. Tell the children what it is. Then pass the bowl around the group. Have each child take a piece of the ingredient. S/he should smell the ingredient and then taste it. After they have done this, talk about whether they liked the ingredient or not. Do this with each of the fresh ingredients except the sausage.

Now that they are familiar with the fresh ingredients, you can begin creating your pizzas. While the children make their own pizza out of felt, you make a real pizza. First, pass the 'pizza dough' (the 9" circles you made) to each child. You keep the real dough. Then pass out the red circles. Talk about putting tomato sauce on. As the children put their 'tomato sauce' on, you spread the real sauce on the pizza dough. Next put on the cheese. Pass around the felt 'sausage pieces'. If a child wants sausage on his/her pizza then s/he should take several pieces and put them on the pizza. At the same time you add sausage to the real pizza. Pass another ingredient, let the children take it and continue to create their pizza. Continue to build the real and felt pizzas. When everyone is finished, put the real pizza in the oven and bake it. While it is cooking, let each child tell what ingredients s/he put on the pizza s/he made. When the pizza is finished, eat it for a snack or lunch.

Create a pizza

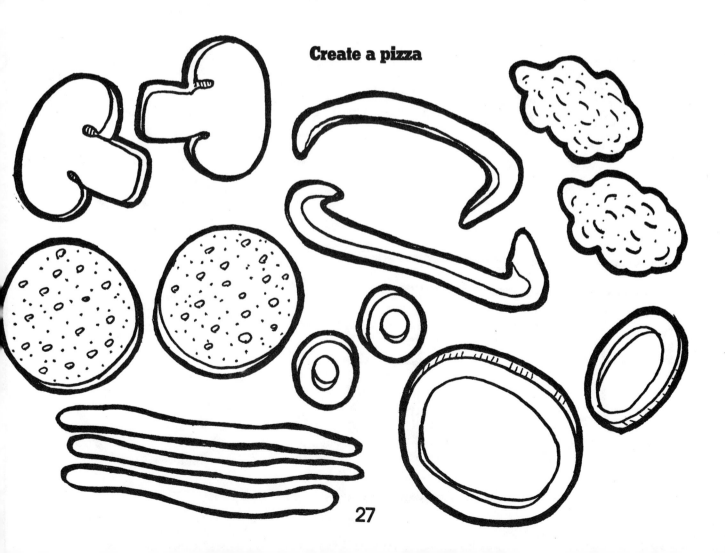

33

Dress the scarecrow

34

35

MY FEELINGS

Make

Happy face
Sad face
Angry face
Sleepy face
Hurt face
Surprised face
Scared face

My looking glass: Say this rhyme with the children. Have the children pretend they are looking into a mirror and have them make the appropriate feeling face as they say the poem.

MY LOOKING GLASS
I looked into my looking glass
And what kind of a face did I see?
I saw a happy face looking back at me.
I guess I am happy today.
(Change the feelings and repeat several times.)

Once the children are familiar with the words of the rhyme, put the feeling faces on the board. Now repeat the rhyme, but this time, point to the feeling face rather than say it. The children should look at the feeling face and complete the rhyme. As before, they should also pretend to look in a mirror and portray the emotion into it.

Make

Body to go with
   the feeling faces
Use the feeling faces
   from the activity MY
   LOOKING GLASS

Props

Small non-breakable
   hand mirror for
   each child

How do I look: Put the body with one feeling face on the board. Have the children call out the name of the feeling which is portrayed. Switch faces and call out that feeling. Continue until the children have identified all of the feelings.

Give each child a mirror. Put one of the feelings on the body again. Have the children portray that feeling into the mirror. Talk about how their faces feel while they are portraying that particular emotion. Change the face on the felt board and repeat the activity.

Make

Use the feeling
   faces from the
   activity MY
   LOOKING GLASS

Name that feeling: Put all of the feeling faces on the board. Tell the children various short stories, each portraying a distinct feeling. When you are finished with the story, ask the children how a certain person in the story felt. Talk about why they think the person felt that certain way. Once you have discussed how that person felt, find the face/s that look/s like that feeling/s. Here are a few stories with which to begin:

Philip was riding his tricycle around the block. He started out riding slowly. Soon he began to pedal faster and faster. When he turned the corner, his trike fell over, and he fell off.

Carol is four years old today. Her mom and dad have planned a birthday party for her. She is going to have four friends over for games and birthday cake.

Catherine was playing with her favorite set of colored blocks. Carin came over and began playing with the blocks without asking Catherine. Catherine's building got destroyed.

MY FEELINGS

Make

Use the feeling
faces from the
activity MY
LOOKING GLASS

Point to the feeling: Put all of the feeling faces on the felt board. Point to each face and have the children name the primary feeling being portrayed. Have a child pretend to be 'sad' while you say, *"Jossie feels very sad today. Look at Jossie and then at all of the feeling faces. Staying where you are, point to the one you think is Jossie's sad face."* Let everyone point to the one that they think looks like Jossie. You purposely touch the wrong face and say *"This one?"* The children say *"No!"*. Point to another one or two faces that the children will recognize as incorrect and will say *"No!"*. Then point to the sad face and the children will agree with you. Now that you have agreed on which one is Jossie's 'sad' face, have the children discuss different reasons why Jossie might be feeling 'sad' today. Continue doing this activity with other feeling faces.

Make

Large tree with
   branches
Photos backed with
   felt

Feeling photos: During free play take a photograph of each child as s/he pretends to have a certain feeling. After the photos are developed and backed with felt, enjoy making a *'feeling tree'* with the children.

Put the bare tree on the felt board. One at a time hold up each child's photo. Have him/her come up and get the photo. When everyone has his/her own picture, have a child stand, hold up his/her picture, and tell what feeling s/he was portraying. Then let several others tell when they have felt that way in a real situation. Have the child hang his/her feeling photo on a branch of the tree. Continue by letting each child tell about his/her feeling photo and then others sharing experiences when they really felt that emotion.

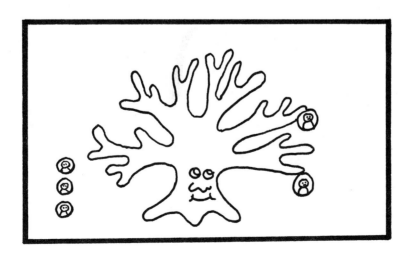

MY FEELINGS

Make

Grumpy Mr. Jones
Sleepy Mrs. Jones
Happy Mardi
Sleepy Heather
Crying Willie
Singing face
Startled face
Mad face
Sly face
Silly face

The Jones family: Tell the children this tale about the town of 'Feelings'. Put the individual faces near the top of the board. Have the characters in front of you and add them when they are first introduced into the story.

It was a strange day in the town called 'Feelings'. Everyone woke up feeling differently than usual. Take for example the Jones family. Mr. Jones was usually grumpy first thing in the morning, but this morning he woke up singing one of his favorite songs, 'Old MacDonald Had A Farm'. (Ask the children to find the singing face that Mr. Jones had that morning. Put it over his grumpy face. Then ask the children how it feels when they're singing. After a short discussion, sing 'Old MacDonald Had A Farm'.)

Now Mrs. Jones usually woke up feeling really sleepy. It often took her about fifteen minutes to wake up. But today she was wide awake. There had been a loud noise which startled her and she jumped up very wide-eyed. (Have the children put the wide-eyed, startled face over Mrs. Jones' sleepy face. Talk about what the loud noise could have been.)

There were three children in the Jones family. Mardi was the oldest. She was nine. Most of the time she woke up so happy. She liked school and looked forward to going each day. But today things did not go right. She went to get dressed and her clothes were not in the closet. She got mad. (Put her mad face over her happy face.) *She thought she would miss the school bus. Just at that moment her sister Heather came into the room. Heather was usually sleepy in the morning like her mom, but not today. This morning Heather had a very sly, tricky look on her face. Can anyone guess why Heather might have had that look on her face?* (Put the sly face on Heather and talk about why she was feeling tricky.) *Willie was their baby brother. He usually cried first thing to let everyone know he was awake. Like everyone else in his family, Willie was not feeling his normal self. Instead of crying he was making silly faces.* (Find his silly face and put it over his crying one.) Let the children enjoy making silly faces at each other.)

Well, as the day continued, the members of the Jones family discovered they were not alone. Everyone who lived in the town of 'Feelings' woke up feeling differently than usual."

Use this story as a 'lead in' to a discussion on how the children feel when they wake up in the morning or after a nap. If they remember, they can also discuss how different members of their family feel when they get up.

My looking glass

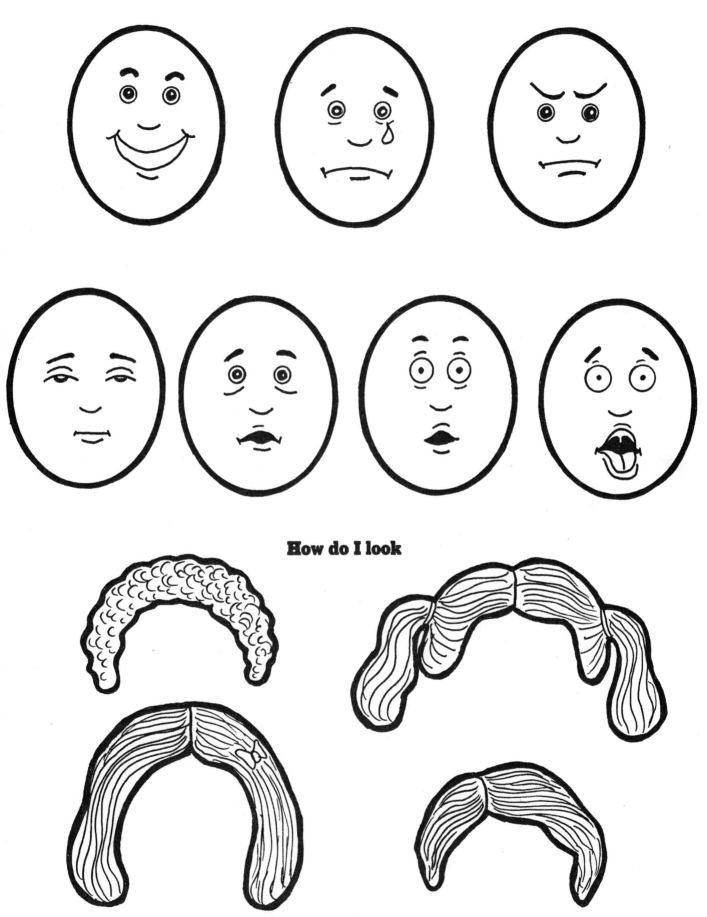

How do I look

39

The Jones family

43

IMAGINATION STRETCHERS

Make

Pictures of people
   backed with felt

Felt puzzles: Hold up one of the pictures for the children to see. Talk about it. Encourage as much detail in their thinking as possible. To do this, ask the children to name the people in the picture, decide how each is feeling and why, predict where each person is going or what they are doing.

    When the children are familiar with the picture, cut it up in enough pieces to challenge them. Put the pieces on the felt board. Have a child come up to the board and put two of the pieces together. Have other children come up and continue adding pieces until the picture is back together.

    Enjoy this activity with all of the puzzles you have made.

Make

Dog
2 girls facing each
   other
2 boys facing each
   other
Several ducks in a
   pond
An apple tree
Ball
Doll
Twig

Talk a little, talk a lot: Have two felt children on the board facing each other as if they were talking. Add one other piece such as the apple tree. Say to your group of children, *"These two children are talking about the apple tree. What do you think they are saying about it?"* When the children have finished, switch the felt children and pieces around and let your children enjoy creating another conversation.
VARIATION: Put one of the felt children and the dog on the board. Say to your group, *"The dog and child are trying to decide what game to play. Let's help them out. What games could they play?"* (Add the ball or twig if it would stimulate their creativity.)

Props

Piece of heavy yarn
   about 3 feet long
A copy of the book IT
   LOOKED LIKE
   SPILT MILK by
   George Shaw

Yarn designs: Make a design with yarn on the felt board. Ask the children, *"What does this design look like?"* Let each of them express their opinion. Some children may want to come up to the board and show you how their idea is incorporated into the yarn. Take the yarn design off of the board and have the children cover their eyes while you rearrange it. Have them open their eyes and discover new objects within the yarn configuration.

    Once the children understand the activity, let them make the designs for their friends. After letting several children create the yarn configurations, read the book, IT LOOKED LIKE SPILT MILK by George Shaw.

Make

Pair of gym shoes
Pair of dress shoes

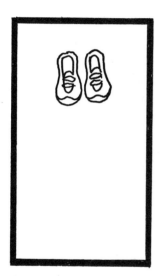

New shoes: Getting new shoes is one of the most exciting occurrences in a young child's life. Say to the children, *"Can you remember when you got a new pair of gym shoes?"* Talk a little bit about the experience. Discuss where they got their shoes, if they tried on several pairs, how they chose which pair was exactly right, and so on. Then enjoy this activity:

Put the pair of gym shoes on the felt board. Chant this rhyme,

NEW SHOES
New shoes, new shoes
These shoes are new.
Here are some special things
They can help me do.

Let the children tell each other all of the things that new gym shoes help them do.

Enjoy the activity again on another day, only this time use dress shoes rather than gym shoes. Once again talk about the experience of buying the shoes. Compare this experience to that of buying the gym shoes. Have the children decide if the experiences were similar or different. How? Then say the chant together and discuss all of the activities you can do when wearing new dress shoes. (This may be a little more difficult than gym shoes.) Emphasize the differences and similarities in the activities that they do when wearing gym and dress shoes.

Use other pairs of footwear such as rain or snow boots or slippers.

Make

Baseball - Football
Pail - Shovel
Soap - Bucket of water
Pencil- Paper
Egg - Skillet
Waffles - Syrup
Hammer - Nail - Board
Foot - Shoes - Socks

Going together: Put the first set of felt pieces near the top of the felt board. Point to each piece and have the children call out its name. Then challenge them to figure out why the pieces go together. When a child has an idea of what connects the pieces, have him/her tell the group.

Discuss other reasons why the pieces could be paired. Encourage the children to create as many as possible. When the children have thought about and discussed these pieces put up the next set. Once again try to think of all of the reasons why these particular pieces go together. Continue through the remaining sets. Play this game often, creating new sets with felt pieces you have made for other activities.

Make

Use pieces from other activites.

Going together, Activity II: Put between ten and fifteen different felt pieces on the board. Point to each one and have the children name it. Then say to the group, *"Look at all of the pieces. I'm looking for two pieces that could go together."* For example, *"The duck and the elephant go together because they are both animals."* or *"The twig and the tree go together because they are both hard."* Let the children continue from there, matching pieces that go together and telling why they do. Encourage their imagination as they try to find reasons why different pieces go together. Remember, they can use a piece more than once.

Make

Pieces for a
   Snowman
   Face
   Lamp
   Big wheel
   Wagon

Props

Large sheet of
   butcher paper
Wide marker

Guess what I am: Tape the piece of butcher paper to the wall near the felt board. Have the various sets of felt pieces in front of you. Choose one set. Tell the children that you are going to create a familiar figure with the pieces. They should watch carefully as you add new pieces. When anyone thinks s/he knows what you're creating s/he should tell the others. Write down all of the children's guesses on the butcher paper. When the figure is completed, read over the list and, see if anyone guessed what the figure was before it was finished.

Make

Rectangle for the basic
   shape of a house
Additional shapes
   which coordinate
   with the rectangle to
   complete a house

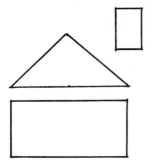

Build a house: Put all of the felt pieces on the board. Point to each one and name the shape. Tell the children that they are going to construct a house with the pieces. First have them close their eyes and try to picture a house that they see on their way to or from school. As they have their eyes shut, stir their imagination with questions. How many windows does the house have? Where is the door? Are there windows in the door? How do you open the door? Is the roof flat or triangular shaped? Are there stairs going up to the front door?

   Once they have had several minutes to think about how the house is constructed, have them open their eyes and look at the felt shapes once again. Point to four or five pieces. Talk about what those pieces could be used for — such as squares could be windows, a small circle might be a door knob, and so on. Then ask them, *"What shape should we use first?"* Have a child come up, pick one, and tell the others why s/he chose that one. Continue from here, adding and changing pieces as the children's ideas develop.

Make

Use familiar characters from other activities such as Mr. Puffin from the COLORS section.

Create a story: Tell the children that they are going to have the opportunity to 'make-up' a story. Introduce the character you have chosen, for example Mr. Puffin. Before you begin encouraging the children to create the story, talk about the balloon man. Give him a name, discuss what he is wearing, talk about his job, speculate on whether he has a family, who is in the family, and any other thoughts that would give the children information to help them be able to create a story.

When you think that the children are ready to begin, introduce the activity. First explain to them that you are going to tape their story as they 'make it up'. Then they will be able to hear it again later. You begin the story and then let the children continue it.

"It was a beautiful day in the summer and the balloon man, Mr. Puffin, was ready to sell balloons to all of the children and adults who were enjoying the animals at the zoo. He had many colorful balloons for people to buy. The first family came up to Mr. Puffin. Each of the children picked out a balloon. Amy the oldest child picked a _____." Let the children continue the story from this point. As it goes on, you will need to encourage and guide the story without stifling the children's thinking. (The more you do this type of activity, the less directing you will be required to do and the more the children are able to think clearly and creatively. Remember, they are new at this, the stories may be short and illogical in the beginning. Throughout the year the children will learn the necessary skills.)

EXTENSION: After the story has been created, help the children make felt pieces which would enhance the story. Several days later, have the children tell the story again using the felt pieces which they developed.

New shoes

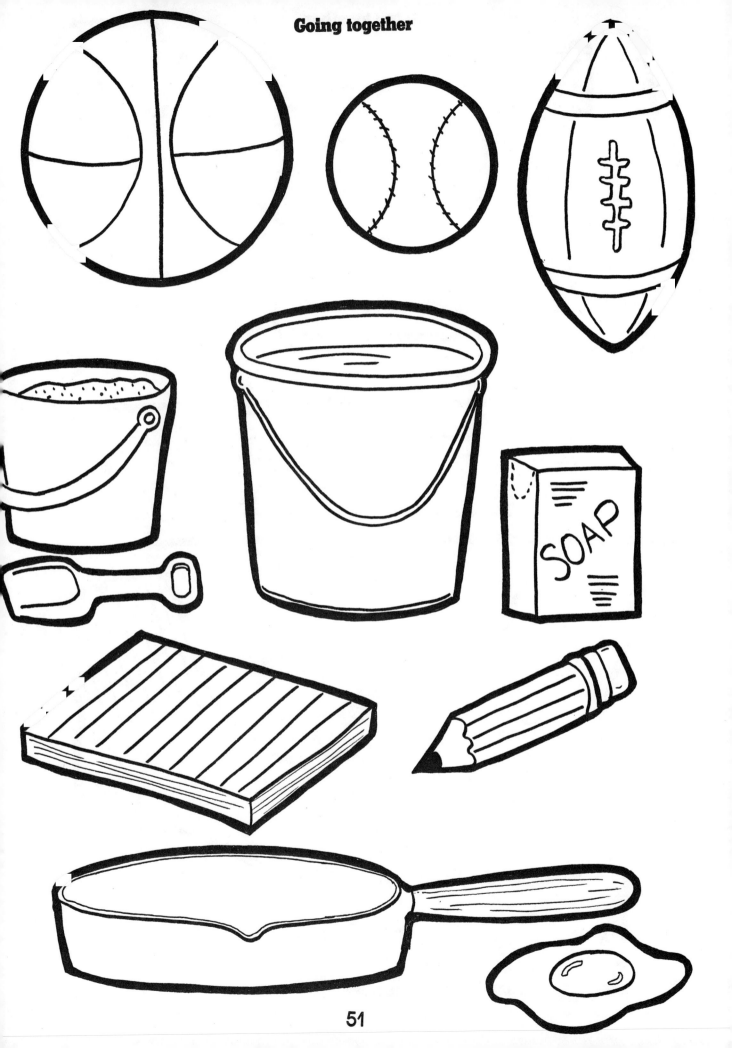

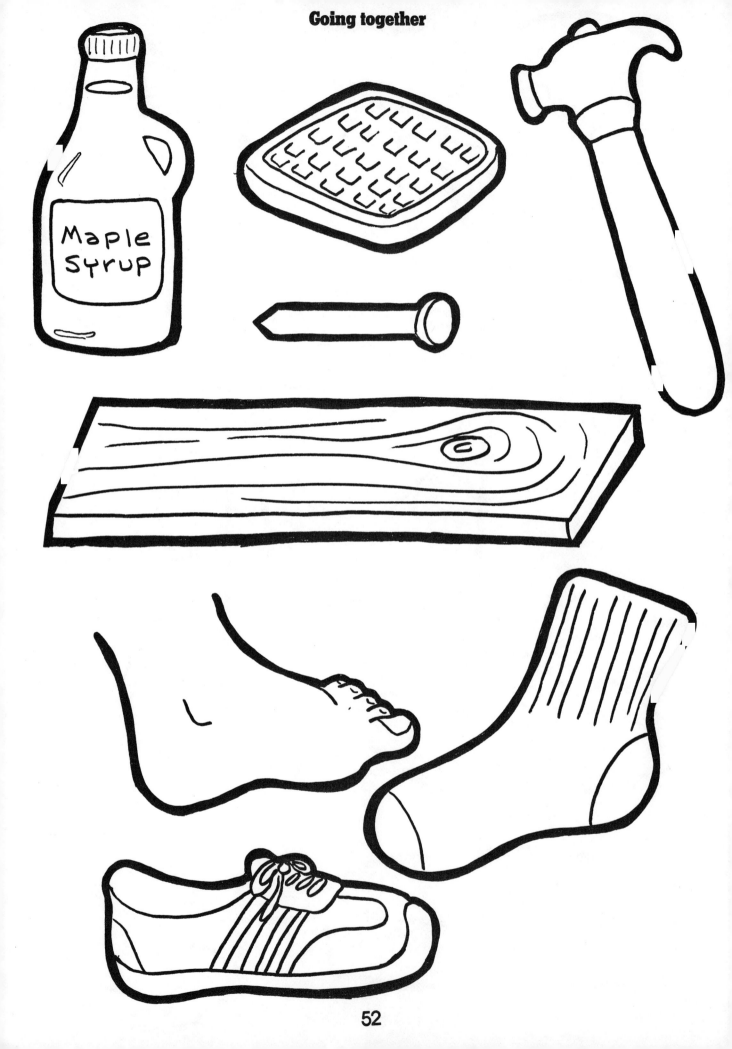

Guess what I am

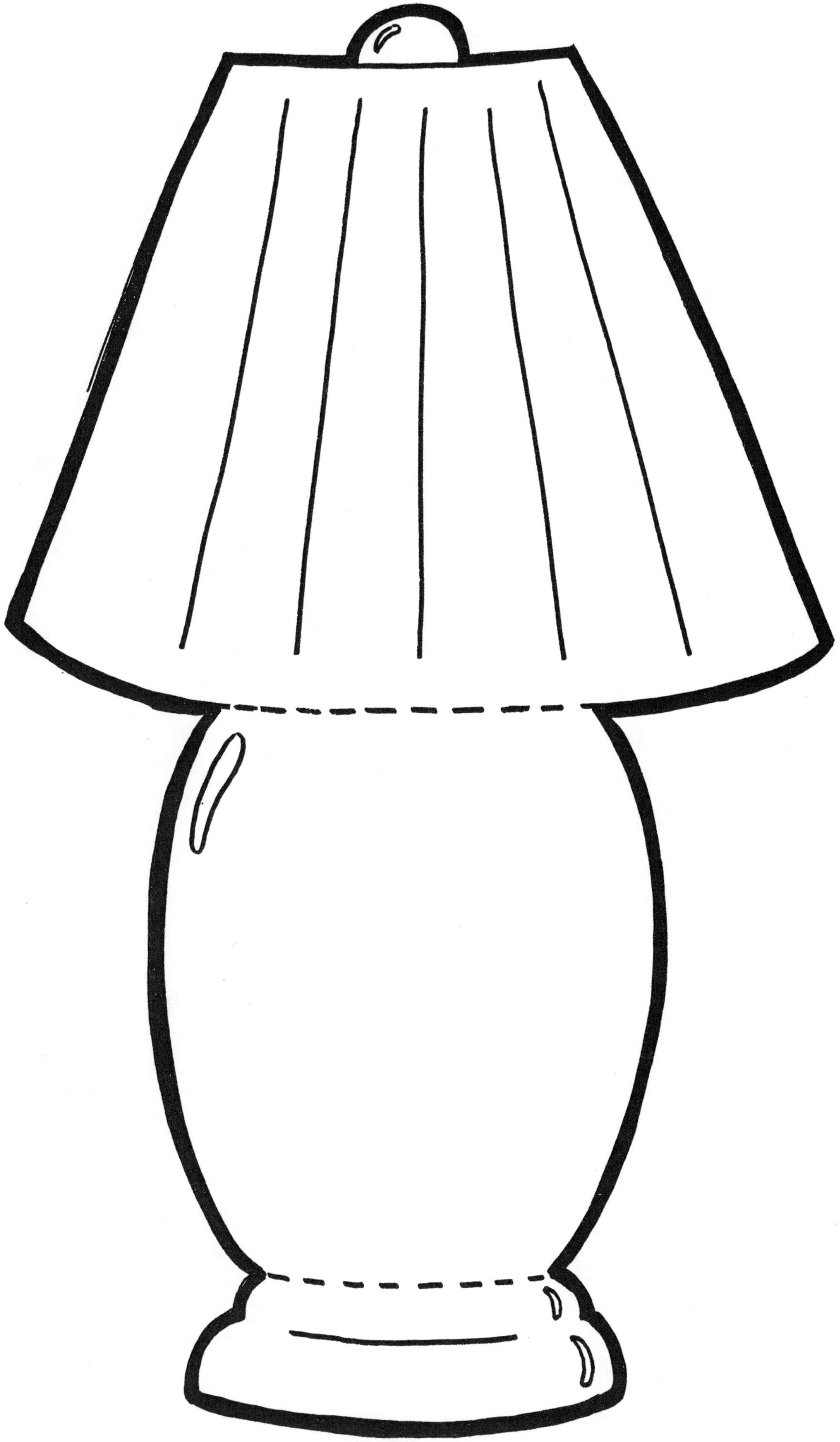

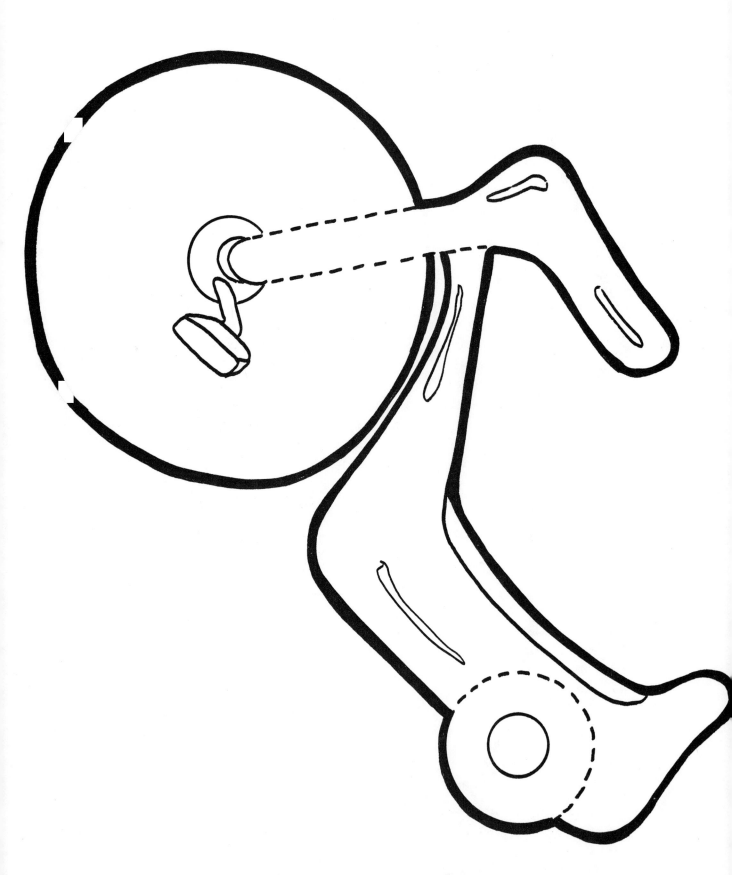

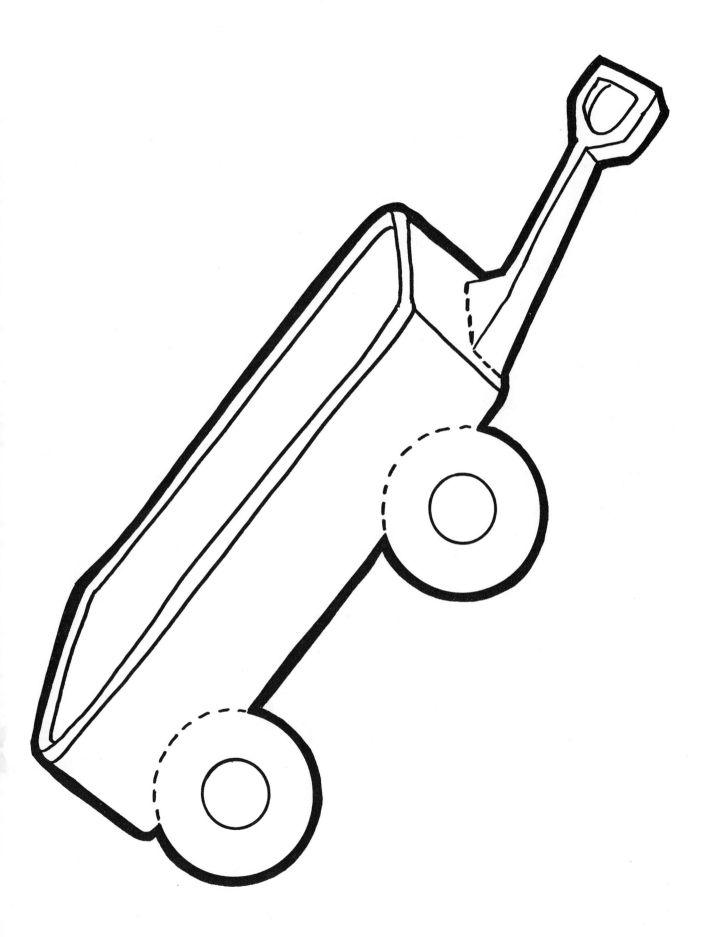

SEASONS
SUMMER

Make

10 different
bathing suits,
some for boys
and some for
girls — more
suits than you
have children in
your group.

Props

Piece of yarn
the width of
your felt board

Swimsuit sale: Pretend that the felt board is Murphy's Children's Store. In the store is a rack with children's swimming suits hanging on it. These suits are 'on sale'. Put the piece of yarn across the top of the felt board. Hang all of the suits on the rack. Have one child be the customer and the other children be the clerks. When the customer comes into the store looking for a suit, s/he should stand in front of the suits and describe, without pointing, the suit s/he wants. All of the 'clerks' listen to the description. When any of the 'clerks' recognize the suit being described, s/he goes up to the rack and hands the suit to the customer. If it is the correct suit, the customer pays the clerk. If it is not, the customer says, *"Not that one."* and continues to describe the suit until s/he gets the one s/he wants. Have the children take turns being customers in the shop. Continue until all of the swimming suits have been sold.

Make

Black bird
Blue bird
Red bird
Yellow bird
Green bird
Matching birdhouses
for each color of
bird

Find your birdhouse: Begin the activity by saying, *"It is summer and all of the birds are enjoying the warm weather. They are flying around, diving to the ground, playing tag in the air, and so forth."* (Have the children pretend they are birds enjoying the summer sun.)

When the children are back in the group, put the felt birds on the upper part of the board as if they were in the sky. As you do this, have the children quietly call out the various colors of the birds. Then say to the children, *"It is close to evening and the birds know they must go home. Not only is it getting dark, but the birds are hungry. What do you think they will have for dinner?* (Discuss this.) *The birds want to be sure that they get back to the right house.* (Line the birdhouses up near the bottom of the board.) *How will the birds know which birdhouse is their own?"* When the children have discovered a way for the birds to find their appropriate homes, have a child come up and fly one of the birds to the correct house. Continue until all of the birds have been safely flown home.

SUMMER

Make

Grey squirrel-brown tail

Black skunk-white stripe

Brown robin-red stomach

Tan rabbit-white nose

Yellow butterfly-brown stripes

Red lady bug- black dots

White duck-orange beak

Sit quietly: Have the children pretend that it is a warm summer day. They are sitting in a park, forest preserve or their back yard watching many small animals scampering around, racing up and down the trees, and flying in the air.

Have the children pick a place where they would like to sit and watch. Go around the group and have them tell everybody where their spot is. Then pass out the animals to some of the children and the features to other children. Have one of the children with an animal come up and put it on the felt board. Have him/her tell the others what animal s/he just saw as s/he was sitting quietly. Then have the child who is holding that animal's feature come up and add it. For example, the first child would bring up the skunk and say, *"I was sitting in the park and I saw a skunk."* The second child would bring up the white stripe and lay it across the skunk's back. Continue until all of the animals are on the felt board.

When all of the animals are on the board, make a clapping noise and say, *"Oh, that noise startled all of the animals. They are all going away."* Name each animal and have one of the children give it to you. When all of the animals have left, say to the children, *"All of the animals are gone, let's go home for lunch."*

FALL

Make

Squirrel
Leaf
Cherry tree
Rake
Acorn
Tree blowing in the wind
Pumpkin

What am I: There are many signs for each season. Fall is probably one of the most colorful, due to the multitude of ripe fruits and vegetables as well as the changing appearance of the countryside. Put five or six of the fall signs on the board. Say a short, descriptive sentence about one of the fall signs, such as, *"I turn all different colors in the fall."* or *"I store my food now so I will not be hungry in the winter."* or *"People use me to help keep their yards clean."* After each description, have a child come up to the board and point to the sign you just described. As s/he points to the sign, have the group call out its name.

Make

4 or 5 varieties of leaves cut from different colors of felt
Large wheelbarrow
Large trash can

Cleaning up the leaves: Have the pile of leaves in front of you. Put the wheelbarrow on the felt board. Talk about the different things for which wheelbarrows are used. Then begin to fill the wheelbarrow with the various colored leaves. As you put the leaves in the wheelbarrow, have the children call out the color of each leaf.

When all of the leaves are in the wheelbarrow say, *"Let's push the wheelbarrow over to the trash can and dump the leaves in it so they can be picked up on garbage day.* (Put the trash can on the board. Have the children help fill it up.) *Aaron, come up and take all of the red leaves out of the wheelbarrow and put them into the trash can."* Continue asking different children to put specific colored leaves into the trash can.

Pretend that the strong fall winds blew the trash can over and all of the leaves blew out. Have the children help refill the trash can.

FALL

Make

Twigs
Rocks and stones
Use various leaves
    from the activity
    CLEANING UP THE
    LEAVES
Use the acorn from
    the activity WHAT
    AM I
Other signs of fall
    appropriate to your
    locale

Props

Plastic tubs for each
    type of thing the
    children would have
    found on their walk
1 paper plate for
    each child

Make

Use the 3-4 leaves
    from the activity
    CLEANING UP THE
    LEAVES
Several of each
    Pair of legs
    Pair of arms
    Pair of eyes
    Mouth
    Nose
    Faces
    Hats

Fall scavenger hunt: On a lovely fall day enjoy a hike to a near-by park or play area in your neighborhood. Let each child carry a small paper bag which s/he has decorated at art. While walking, encourage the children to pick up a variety of things which remind them of fall.

When you return to the center have the children bring their bags to the circle time area. Give each child a paper plate and have him/her dump the 'goodies' onto it. Then put one of the fall signs on the felt board, for example the acorn. Have the children name it. Then walk around the circle with one of the plastic tubs. Let the children put all of the acorns which they found on their walk into the tub.

Next display one of the leaves. Name the type of leaf it is. Talk about its particular shape and size. Once again walk around the circle and let the children put that type of leaf into another tub. Continue until all of the items have been sorted into different tubs.

EXTENSION: Put the tubs in the Discovery Area of your classroom so the children can examine the fall signs more closely during free play.

Leaf people: Put three or four different leaves at the top of the felt board and the features off to the side. Tell the children that they are going to create people using the leaves as the body. Have one child come up to the board and pick the leaf for the first leaf person. Have him/her put the leaf in the center of the board. Have other children continue creating the person by picking various features and adding them to the leaf. Create a second and third leaf person in the same way. When you've finished creating several people, go back and give each one a name.

EXTENSION: Take a walk and have each child find a leaf. Create leaf people as an art activity using markers or paint for the features and the leaf for the body.

WINTER

Make

Child
Snowpants
Jacket
Scarf
Hat
Gloves
Boots

Let's get dressed: *"It's time for the children to go outside and play in the snow. Everyone is so excited because it snowed during the night. Several children are planning to build a snowman, two children are going to make angels in the snow, others are going to look for animal tracks, and still others are going to roll down the hill near the back of the play area. Before anyone can go outside, however, each person has to put on all of his/her snow clothes."*

Put the felt child and the snow clothes on the board. Dress the child for snow play. As you dress the felt child, talk about the order in which the snow clothes go on.
EXTENSION: As your children get ready to go outside into the winter weather, refer to the order in which the felt child got dressed. Have them put their snow clothes on in the same order.

Make

Quilt
Fire
Coat
Sweater
Hot drink
Bed
Hat
Scarf
Mittens
Several strips of white
    paper backed with
    felt

Keeping warm: Have the children pretend it is a cold winter day. BRRRRRR!! Then have them think of all of the different ways that they can use to become warm. Have the felt pieces in an envelope in front of you. As they think of a way, put the felt representation on the board. If they think of a way for which you do not have a picture, write it on one of the white strips and put it on the board. Continue until they have thought of many of the possibilities. Give them clues if necessary.

When all of the ideas are on the board go back and decide which ways keep you the warmest.

Make

Snowman body
Snowman head
Stovepipe hat
Scarf
Pebble eyes
Carrot nose
Raisin mouth
 Twigs

Build a snowman: Put all of the snowman pieces onto the felt board. Say this poem:

> ### LET'S BUILD A SNOWMAN
> *First the body*
> *And then the head.*
> *A stovepipe hat*
> *And a scarf of red.*
> *Pebbles for eyes*
> *And a carrot nose,*
> *A mouth made of raisins*
> *In two smiling rows.*

Say the poem again, but this time say it slowly and have the children build a felt snowman as you go along.

WINTER

Make

Find pictures of snow-related toys in catalogues or magazines. Back each picture with felt.

Props

Have the real toy to match each of the pictures you have found.

Winter toys: Place the pictures of the winter toys on the felt board. Put the real winter toys in the middle of the circle. First let the children identify each of the real toys. Then point to the pictures and have them name the toys pictured in each one. Encourage the children to tell stories about playing with any of the toys.

After all of the children have related their stories, play a matching game. Have a child come up to the felt board, choose a felt piece, tell the others what it is, and then go and stand by the appropriate real toy. Using other children, match each of the pictures to the real toys.

SPRING

Make

Budding tree
Baby raccoon
Baby fox

Kite
Puddle

Sun
Mound of soil
Person gardening
Tractor
Flowers

Raincoat
Rain boots
Umbrella

Signs of spring: Some signs of spring reflect growth and refreshment. Put the budding tree and the baby animals on the felt board. Talk about each one, encouraging the children to relate stories about trees they have seen budding or baby animals which have just been born.

* * * Spring is also a time for flying kites and stomping in puddles. Put the kite and puddle on the board. Encourage the children to tell each other what they do on a rainy day. Do any of them like to go out and stomp in puddles left by a storm? Have any of them flown kites? What happened?

* * * Using the felt pieces, talk about caring for plants in the children's small home gardens and on the large farms. Discuss the fact that seeds and plants need water, sun, soil and care to grow and mature so we have good food to eat. Ask the children if they help their family plant the spring garden.

* * * With the advent of spring, people change the type of clothing they wear. Ask the children what they are wearing now that the weather is getting a little warmer. Put the felt clothes on the board as they name clothes you made. Are these clothes different than the ones they wore in the other seasons? What are the differences? Similiarities?

Make

Butterfly egg
Caterpillar
Coccoon
Butterfly

Props

THE VERY HUNGRY CATERPILLAR, by Eric Carle

Development of a butterfly: Put the felt pieces showing the development of a butterfly on the board. Talk about how the egg develops into a caterpillar, who spins a coccoon and then grows into a beautiful butterfly. In turn the butterfly lays eggs so the cycle will continue and more butterflies will develop. (The best time to do this activity is when the children can see the coccoons hanging from the tree branches or the caterpillars crawling around the sidewalks.)

EXTENSION: Read the book, THE VERY HUNGRY CATERPILLER by Eric Carle. Once again emphasize the four basic stages of a butterfly's development.

SPRING

Make

Carrot with tops
Tomato plant
Cucumber plant
Potato with tops
Green pepper plant
Radishes
Corn
Zucchini

Vegetable garden: Read this rhyme to the children.

VEGETABLE GARDEN

I have a special piece of land
Just outside my door.
It's going to be a garden,
With vegetables galore.

First I planted carrots,
Which grow below the ground,
With bushy green tops above,
They easily can be found.

Next I put tomato plants,
Which grow so very wide.
I'll stake them up to spread them out
So none of them will hide.

Also there are cucumbers,
These I planted in a mound;
So they can grow every which way
Right along the ground.

Finally there are potatoes,
These are funny too.
They grow on roots below the soil
To dig when the summer's through.

If you didn't plant a garden,
I certainly wonder why.
If you don't grow your own vegetables,
Then each one you must buy.

Dick Wilmes

Read the rhyme again, this time putting the vegetables on the board as the rhyme progresses. Talk about what vegetables grow above the ground and which ones grow below the soil. Add more vegetables to each group as you proceed with the conversation.

63

SUMMER

Swimsuit sale

SUMMER

Find your birdhouse

Sit quietly

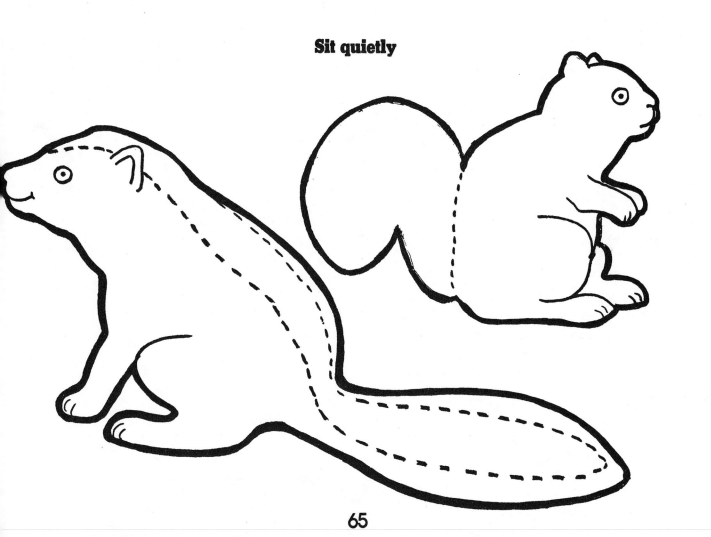

SUMMER

Sit quietly

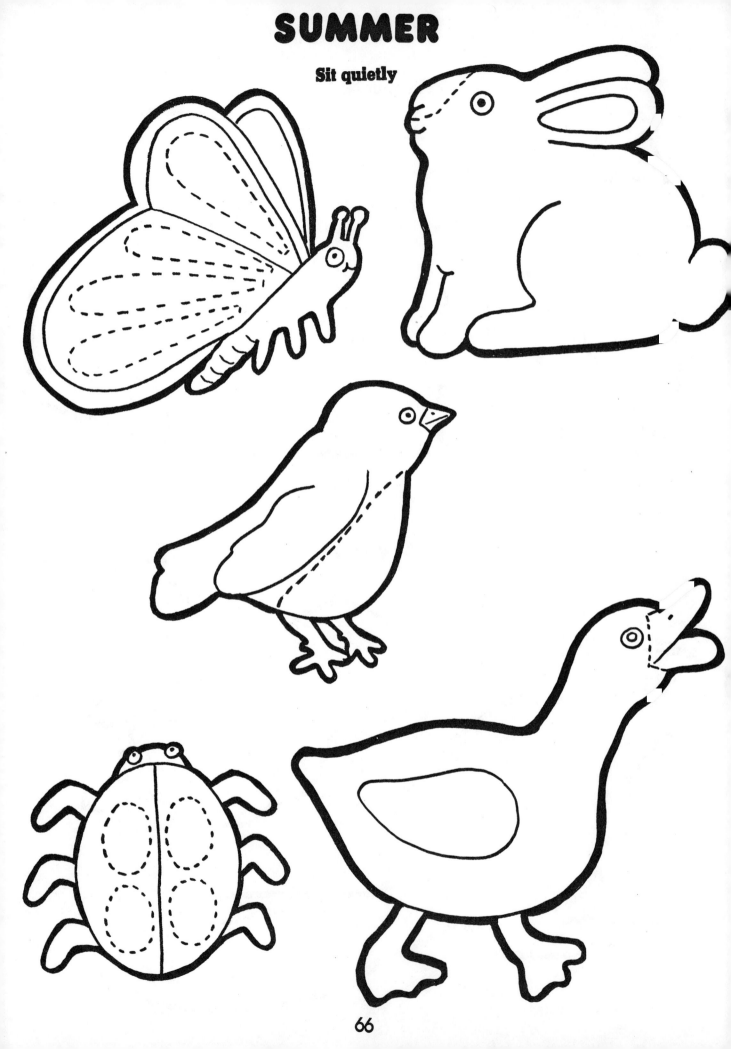

FALL

What am I

FALL

What am I

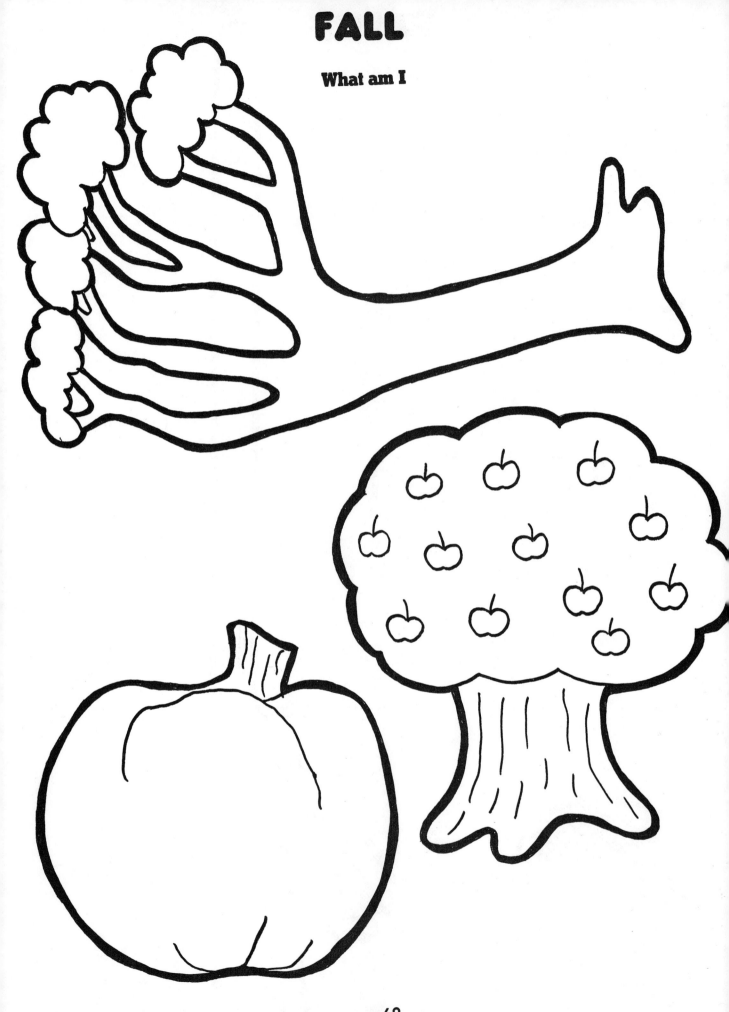

FALL

Cleaning up the leaves

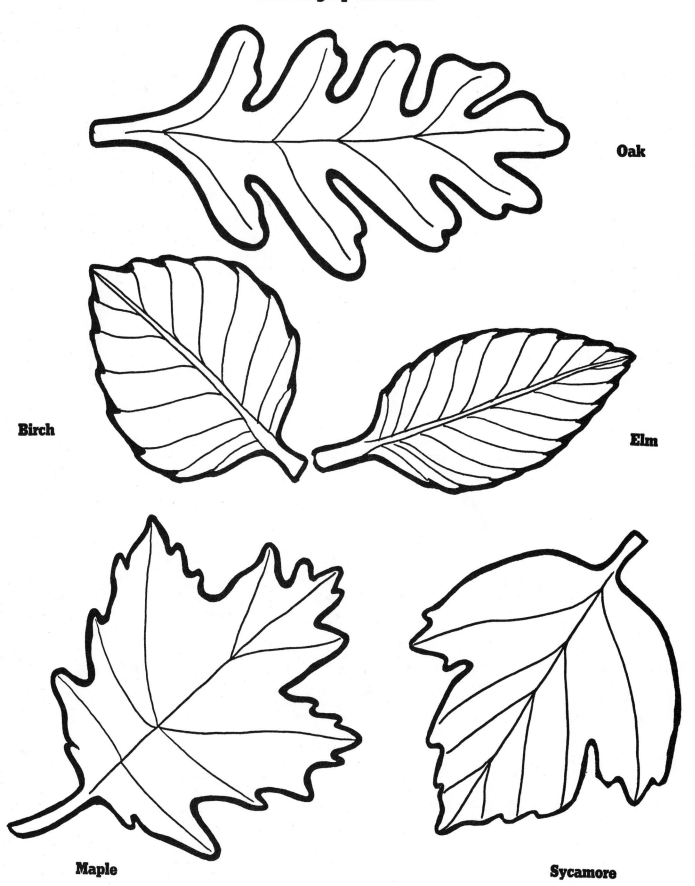

Oak

Birch

Elm

Maple

Sycamore

FALL

Cleaning up the leaves

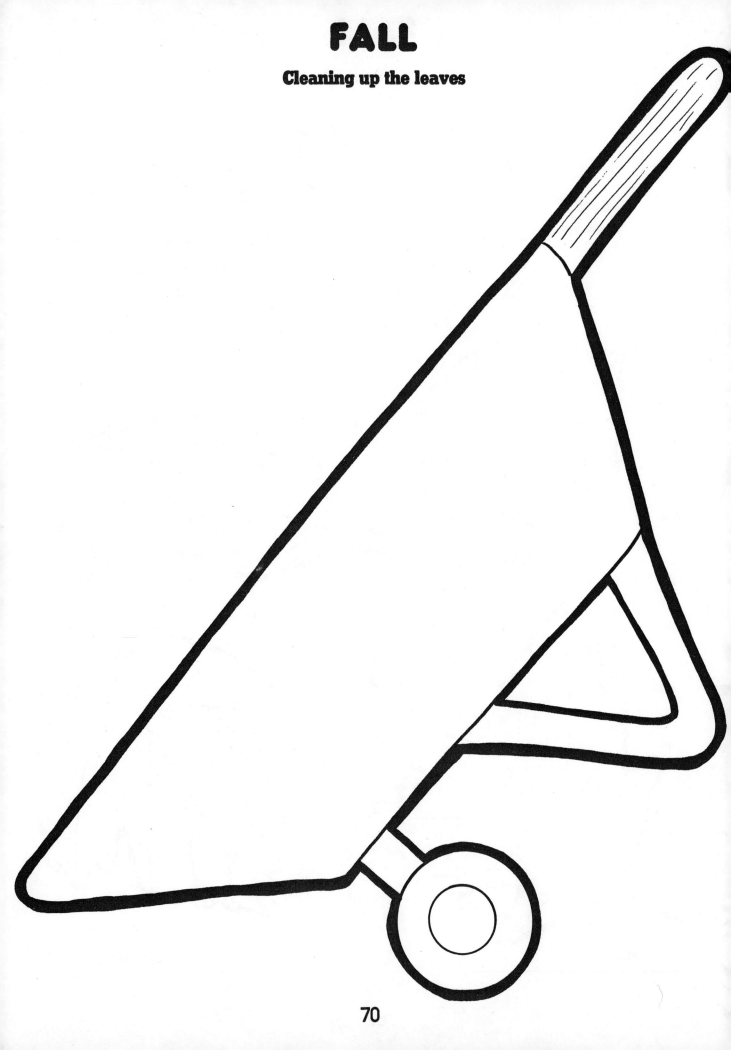

FALL
Cleaning up the leaves

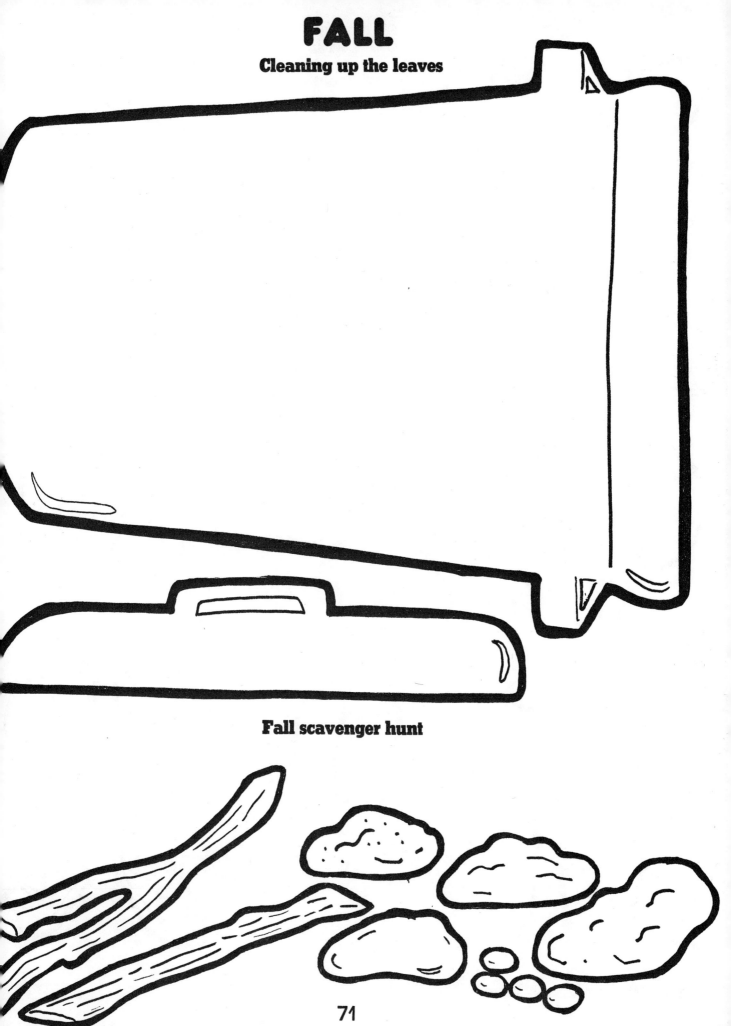

Fall scavenger hunt

FALL
Leaf people

WINTER

Let's get dressed

Boy Pattern on Page 19

Let's get dressed

WINTER
Let's get dressed

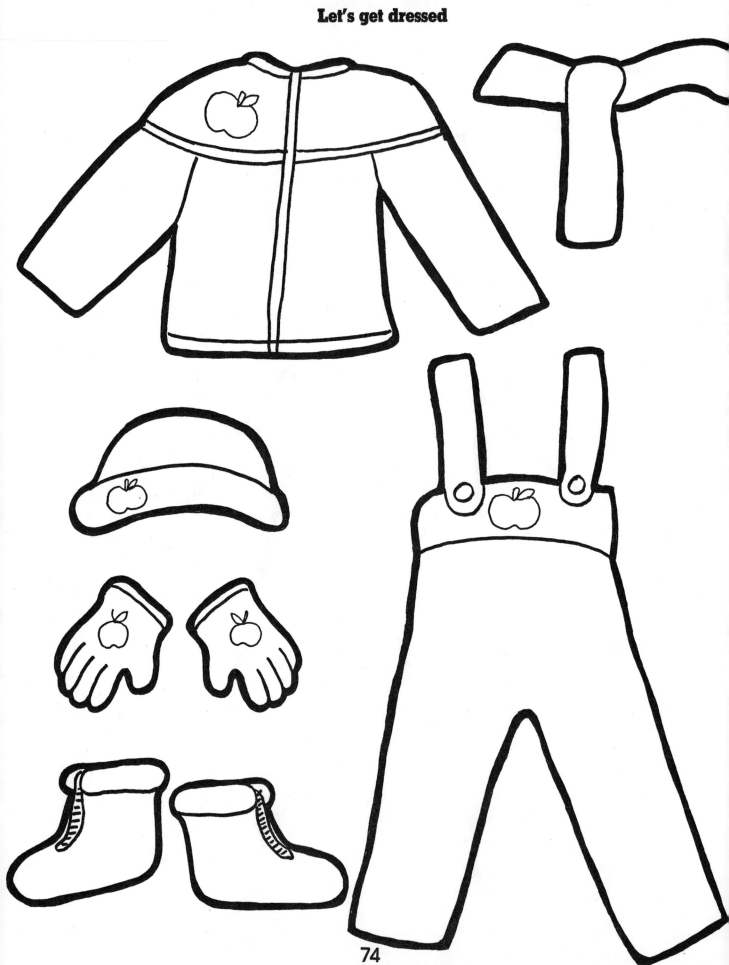

WINTER
Keeping warm

WINTER

Keeping warm

WINTER

Build a snowman

SPRING

Signs of spring

SPRING

Signs of spring

SPRING

Signs of spring

SPRING

Development of a butterfly

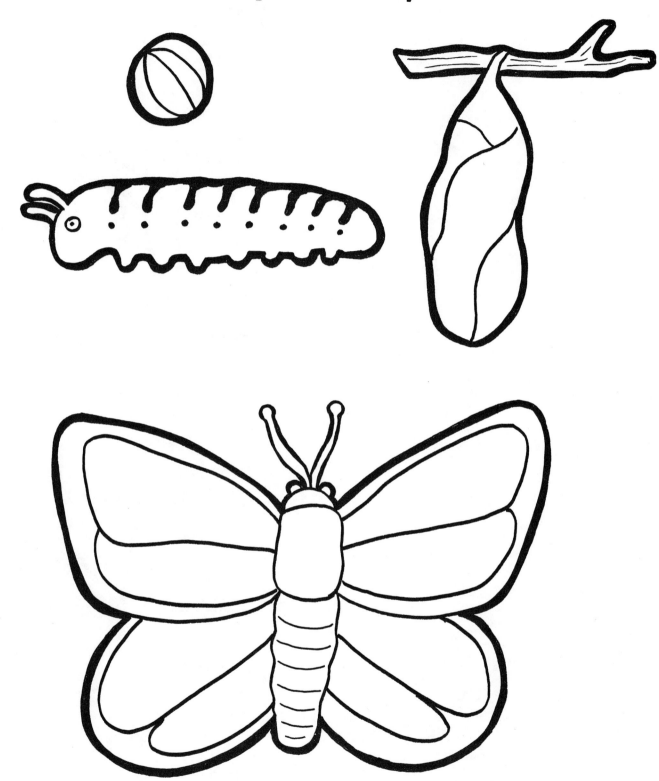

SPRING

Vegetable garden

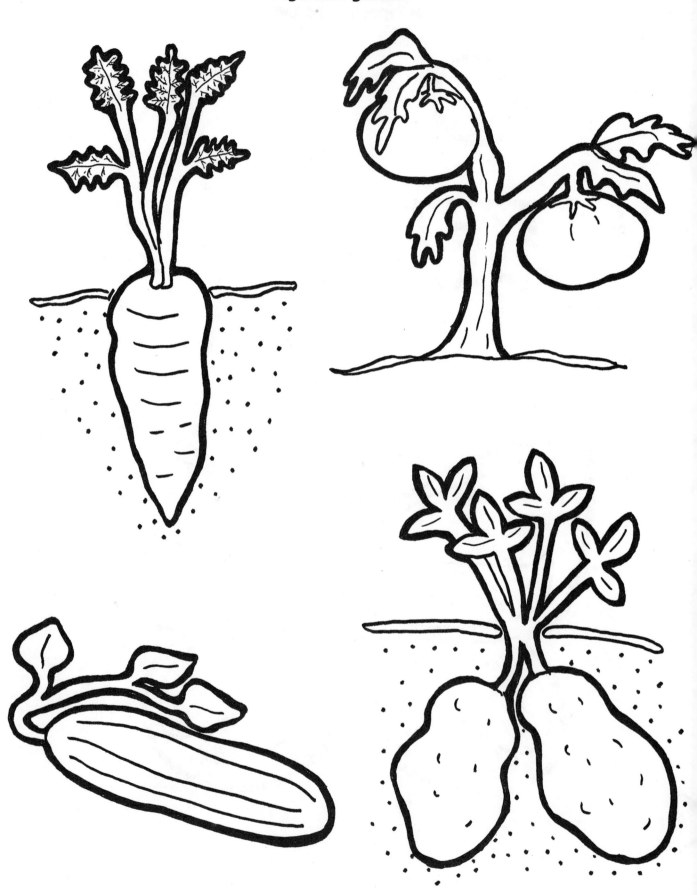

SPRING

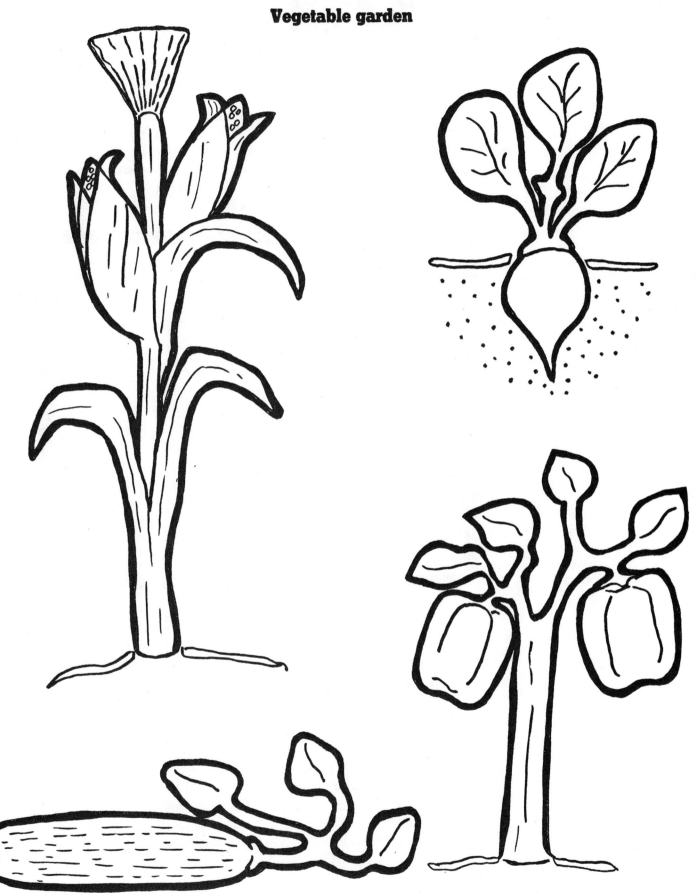

Vegetable garden

FOODS

Make

Vegetables/Fruits
Corn
String beans
Carrots
Lettuce
Cucumber
Apple
Grapes
Grapefruit
Orange
Banana
Strawberries
Melon

Dairy
Milk
Cottage cheese
Yogurt
Cheese

Meats/Fish
Pork chop
Hamburger
Chicken leg
Fish
Eggs

Bread
Wheat bread
Crackers
Noodles
Cereal

Know your food groups: Using the foods from the four food groups, put one from each group at the top of the felt board. Pass the remaining felt pieces out to the children. Point to the first category of food and name it. Have the children look at their food pieces. If they have a food in that category, have them bring it up and put it under the first piece. Continue until all of the foods have been sorted according to their food group. Go back to each group and have the children call out all of the foods in that category.

Make

Dinner plate
Use the foods from the
   activity KNOW
   YOUR FOOD
   GROUPS

A well-balanced meal: Arrange the foods on the board according to the four food groups — breads, fruit and vegetable, meat, fish and poultry, and dairy. After naming each of the foods, talk with the children about the importance of eating a variety of foods during the day. By eating different healthy foods their body will get the nutrition it needs to stay well.

Then put the plate on the board. Challenge the children to create a nutritious meal using the foods that are displayed. Encourage them to use foods from each of the groups. Once they understand how to create a nutritious meal, have them specifically plan a breakfast, lunch, and dinner.

FOODS

Make

Use the foods from the activity KNOW YOUR FOOD GROUPS

What does your family eat: As you put the foods on the felt board, have the children name them.

When you have finished identifying each food, return to the first one and say, *"Do you eat _____ in your family?"* The children will answer. Take this opportunity to discuss like and dislikes in food tastes. It will not only help the children learn more about food, but also about individual differences in tastes and family customs. Continue until you have discussed all of the foods you have on the board. Let the children name other foods they eat in their family.

Make

Picnic basket
Hot dogs
Hot dog buns
Sandwiches
Potato chips
Cupcakes
Hamburgers
Hamburger buns
Pickles
Ketchup
Mustard
Thermos bottle
Plates
Glasses
Silverware
Napkins

Picnic fun: Picnics are one of the most fun activities for all ages. Food, activities, friends, open space and warm sunshine usually blend together to make a memorable day. Talk with the children about the picnics they have been on. Encourage them to talk about the food they enjoyed, the games they played, and the family and friends they were with.

After they have gotten in the 'picnic mood', plan a picnic menu with them. Discuss the foods and accessories they would put in their picnic basket if they were going on a real picnic. Put the basket in the middle of the felt board and the different foods and accessories off to the side. Say *"Let's plan what foods we would like to put in our picnic basket for this afternoon's picnic. Here is our basket and over here are the foods from which we can choose. Before we choose what foods we would like to eat, let's name all of them."* Point to each food and have the children call out its name.

Then begin filling up the picnic basket with the foods they would like to eat. Two ways to do this are to go around the circle or to randomly pick children and have each one pick a food to add to the picnic meal. When s/he tells what food s/he wants, have him/her come up to the felt board and put the food into the basket. When everyone has had the opportunity to put a food into the picnic basket, point to each food, and have the children call out the name of the food.

Once they have chosen all of the foods, have them decide what accessories they will need to set up the picnic. Let them name all of the accessories and then choose the specific ones they will need. Why do they need the ones they selected?

FOODS

Make

Large salad bowl
Lettuce
Tomato
Cucumber
Green pepper
Carrot
Radishes
Several non-salad
   foods from other
   activities

Toss a vegetable salad: Place the salad bowl in the center of the board. Put the 'salad fixings' and other miscellaneous foods off to the side of the bowl. Say to the children *"Let's make a vegetable salad today! Here's the bowl. What is the first thing we need for the salad?"* (Answer) Continue in this manner until all of the salad is prepared.

You should have several foods left on the board that were not used in the salad. Name these foods and discuss why you did not want them in the salad.
EXTENSION: Prepare a real salad for lunch or snack. Use the exact same ingredients you did with the felt salad. As you enjoy the salad, talk about each of the ingredients.

Make

Cooked and uncooked
of each item:
Egg
Oatmeal
Potatoes
Spaghetti
Pancakes
Bacon
And others

Cooked and uncooked foods: Leaving space between each food, put all of the uncooked foods on the board. Pass out the matching cooked foods to the children. Point to each food on the board and have the children identify it. Then call on a child and say, *"Toma, what cooked food do you have?* (Answer) *Put it next to the same uncooked food."* Continue by having each of the children match his/her cooked food with the appropriate uncooked food. As you take the foods off of the board, have the children call out the food names.
EXTENSION: As you prepare snacks and lunches with the children, remember to have them look at all of the ingredients before they are added to the recipe and then again afterwards. Talk about what happens to the ingredients as they are combined together.

Make

Hamburger
French fries
Banana
Hot dog
Corn on the cob
Grapes
Ice cream cone
Pretzels
Mask - 12" square
   piece of felt with a
   2" circle cut in
   the middle of it.

Peek-a-boo foods: Have all of the felt foods in an envelope so that they are hidden from the children. Put the mask on the felt board. Show the children the hole cut in it. Tell them that they are going to cover their eyes and that you are going to slip a picture of food behind the mask. Part of the food will be showing through the opening.

Now have the children cover their eyes. Put a piece of food behind the mask. Then have them open their eyes and look very carefully at what they can see of the food. Can they figure out what the food is? After several children have guessed, take the mask away and look at the entire piece. Had anyone figured it out?

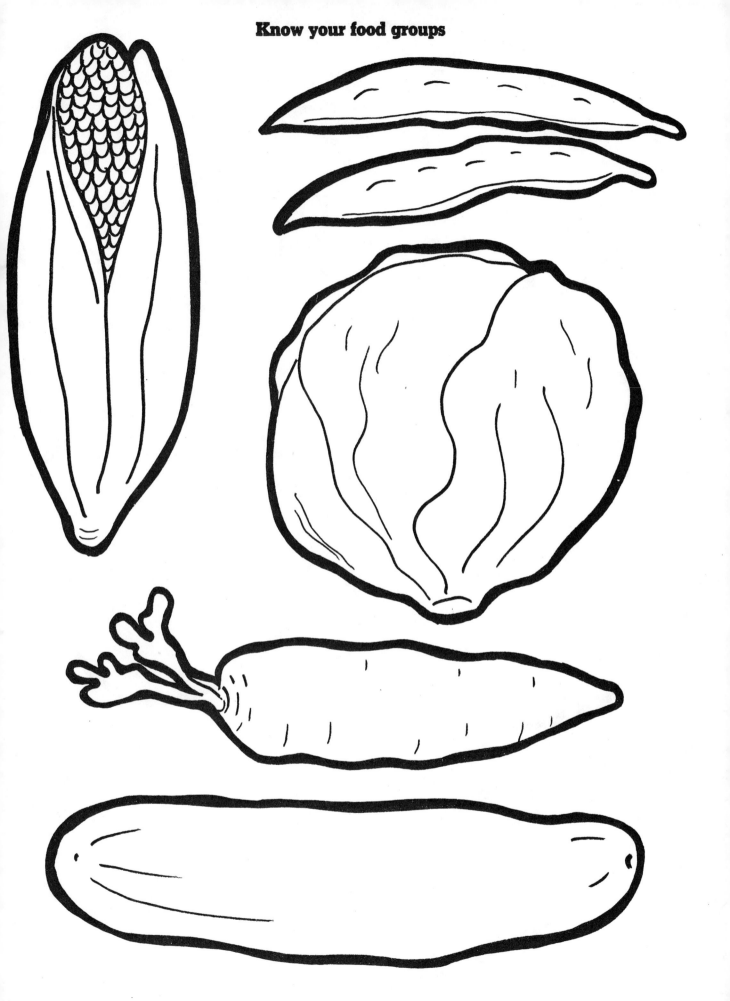

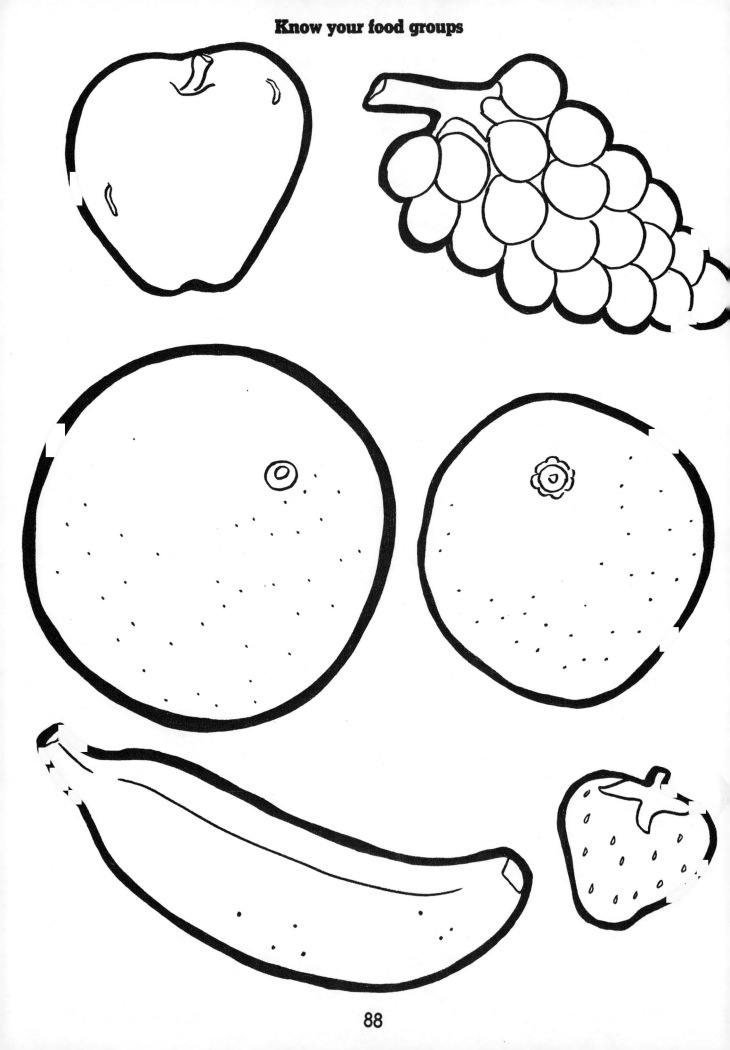

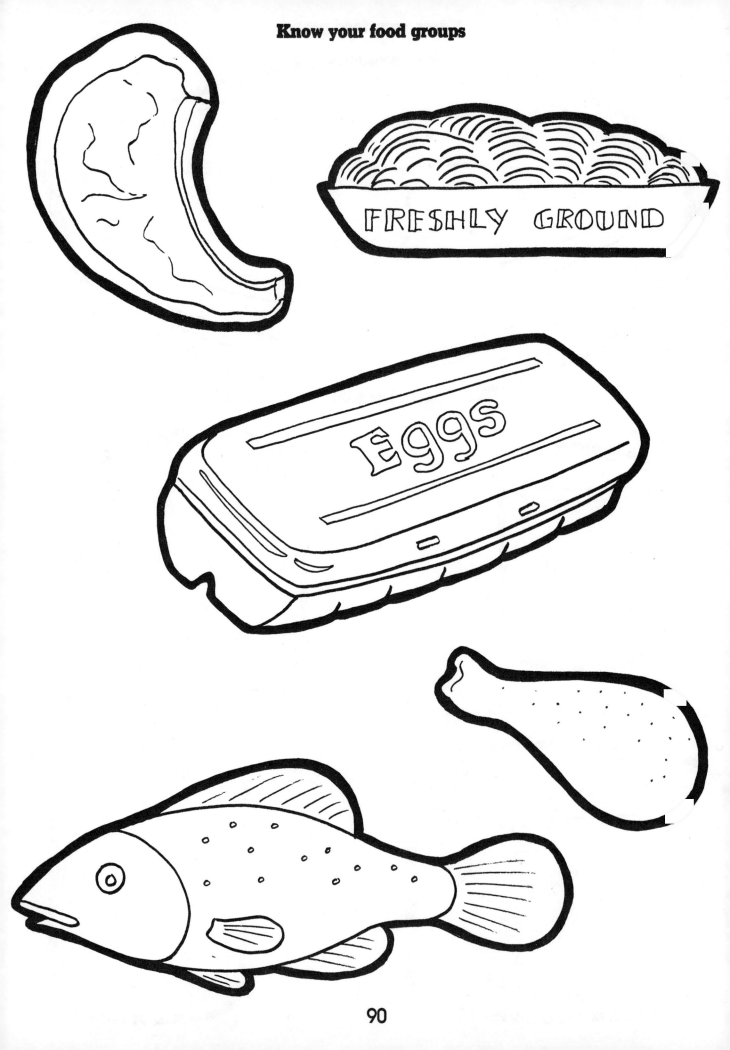

FRESHLY GROUND

Eggs

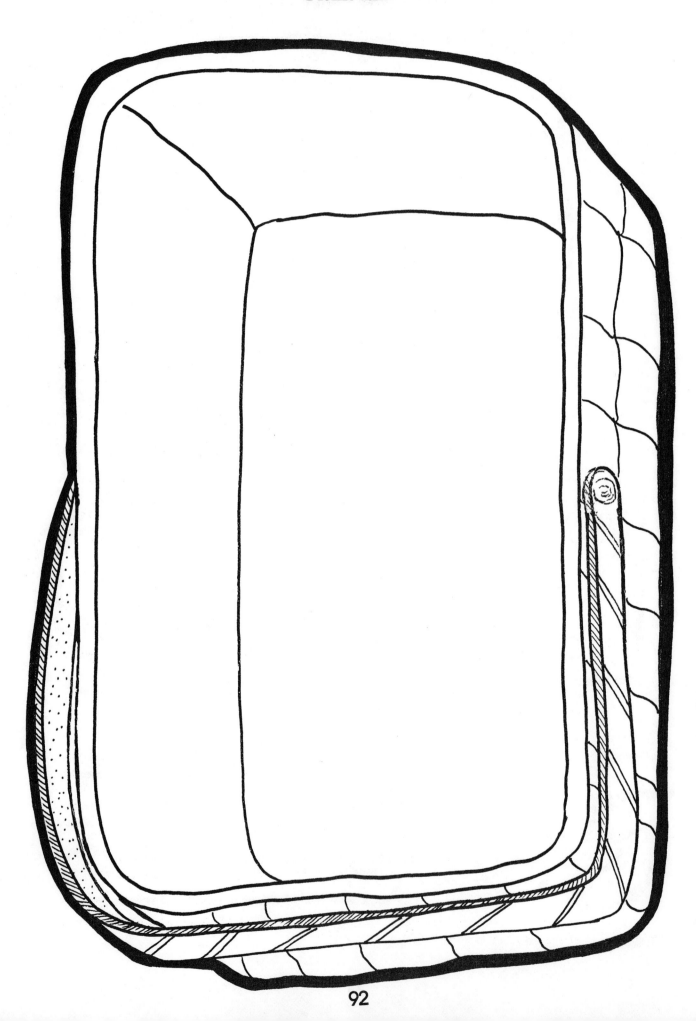

MUSTARD

PICKLES

ketchup

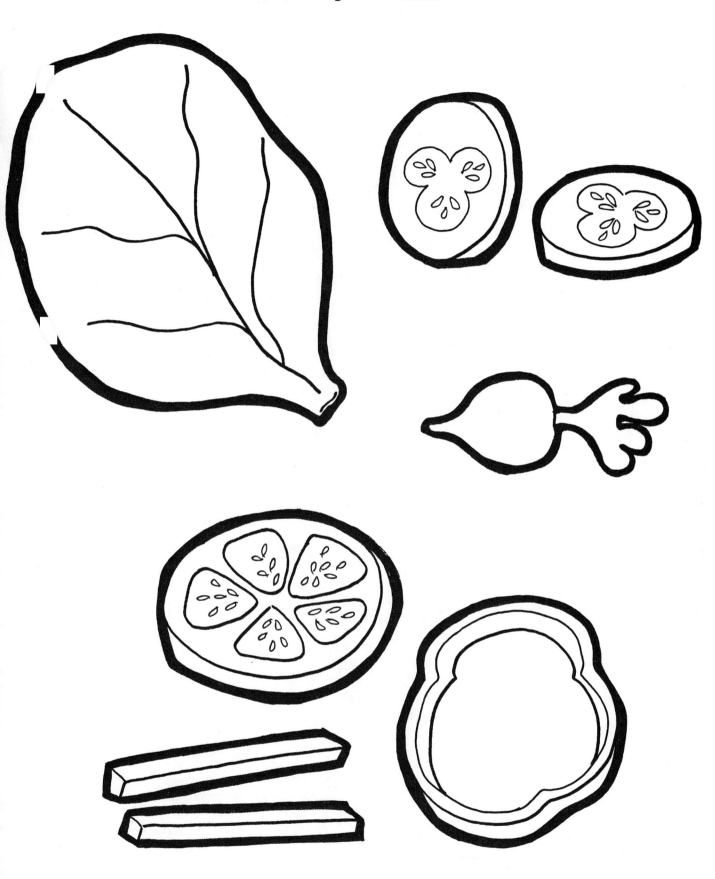

Cooked and uncooked foods

SPaghetti

OATMEAL

You can also use eggs, carrots, hamburgers, and corn patterns.

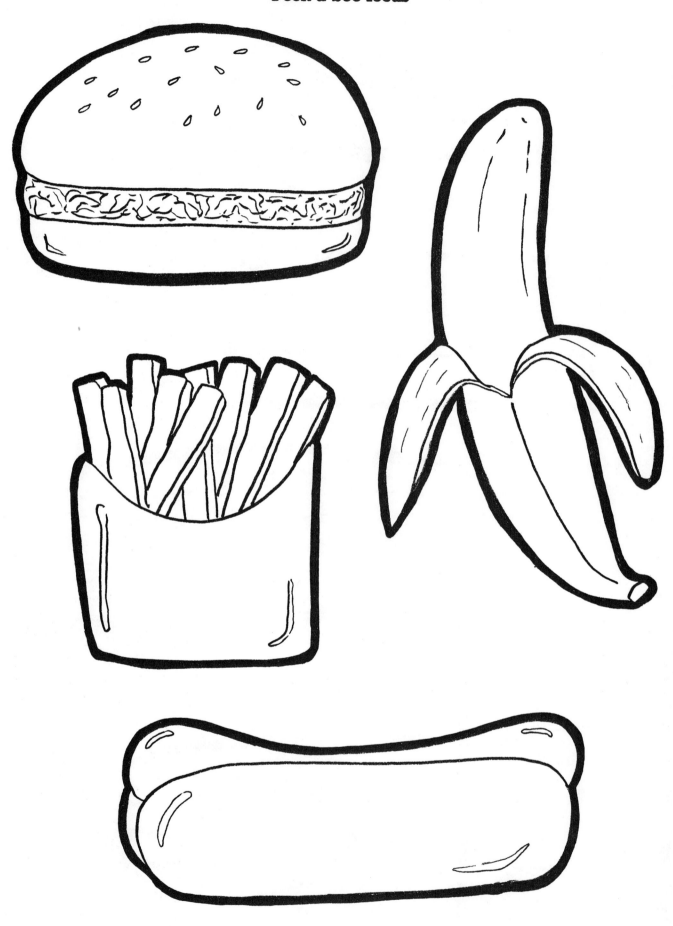

ANIMALS

Make

Bat - Cave
Dog - Doghouse
Spider - Web
Bird - Nest
Butterfly - Coccoon
Ant - Hill
Fish - Water
Seal - Rocks/water

Make

Barn
Cage
House
Cow
Pig
Chicken
Zebra
Elephant
Giraffe
Cat
Use the dog and seal
   from the activity
   NATURAL
   HABITATS

Make

Ostrich
Alligator
Gorilla
Lion
Tiger
Bear
Deer
Hippopotamus
Rhinoceros
Kangaroo
Snake
Use the elephant,
   zebra, and giraffe
   from the activities
   NATURAL
   HABITATS and
   SORT THE
   ANIMALS

Natural habitats: Put all of the animals on the felt board. Pass out the various homes to the children. Point to each animal and have the children identify it by name. Then go back to the first animal and repeat its name and ask who has its home. Let the child who has that animal's home bring it up to the felt board and put the animal in the home. As s/he is putting him in his home have the child tell the others what type of home the animal lives in. When all of the animals are in their natural homes, go back to the first home/animal and challenge the children to think of other animals who live in the same type of home. Continue through all of the animals.

Sort the animals: Put the barn, cage, and house near the top of the felt board. Have the animals in front of you. Hold up an animal for everyone to see. Have the children call out the name of the animal. Let the children decide if this animal lives on the farm, at the zoo, or in a child's home. Give the animal to a child and let him/her put it near the place where the animal lives. Hold up another animal, let the class identify it and have a child put that animal near his home. Continue until all of the animals are home.

Then have the children name all of the animals who live at the zoo, on the farm, or in a child's home.

Animal escape: Pretend the felt board is a zoo. Have as many animals on the board as you have children in the group. Describe one of the animals. Let the children guess which one you are talking about. Have a child come up and help that animal escape from the zoo by taking it off of the board and then bringing it back to his/her seat. Continue until all of the animals have escaped from the zoo.

Play a memory game to help the zoo security police find all of the animals. First go around the circle and have each child name his/her animal. Then have the children put their animal behind them. After that say, *"There was a bear in the zoo. Let's see if we can remember who helped the bear escape."* Let the children guess who has the bear. When they guess correctly, have that child bring the bear back to the zoo. Continue and soon all of the animals will be back in the zoo.

ANIMALS

Make

Use a variety of
  animals from other
  activities in this
  section

Guess who: Have an empty felt board with all of the animals you've chosen in front of you. Say a riddle about one of the animals. Let the children guess which one you're describing. Instead of telling the children if they guessed right, put the animal on the board and the children can see if their answer matches the felt animal.

Make

Use any ten animals
  from other activities
  in this section

Which one is missing: Put ten animals in a line on the felt board. Have a child come up and point to each animal as the group calls out its name. Then have the children cover their eyes. Take one animal off of the board. Have the children uncover their eyes. You say:

> There were ten animals
> Now there are nine
> Guess which one is not in line

Then let the children guess which one is missing. When they guess correctly, put it back. Play again and again. When the children learn the rhyme, have them say it with you before they guess which animal is 'not in line'.

Make

Horse
Sheep
Duck
Rooster
Goat
Use the chicken, cow,
  pig, barn, and
  farmhouse from the
  activities NATURAL
  HABITATS and
  SORT THE
  ANIMALS
Farmer Parsons

Feeding time: Put the barn and the farmhouse on the felt board. Pass out the farm animals to the children. Tell the children that you are going to be Farmer Parsons and 'call in' the animals for feeding. (Put Farmer Parsons on the board.) *"I need to feed all of my animals. It takes me a long time. Will all of you please help me today?* (Answer) *First I want to feed the animals which eat corn. That means I need the chicken, pigs, and sheep.* (Have the children holding these animals put them near the barn.) *The horses are waiting for their hay. Whoever has the horse, please run him to the barn. The roosters and ducks need their seeds. They are all spread out for them just outside the barn. Please bring them in for their daily seeds. The goats and cows are going to eat grass. If you have a cow or goat, just leave him in the pasture. The house pets are last. The dog will eat dog food and the cat wants its milk and cat food. Please bring them to the farmhouse. Thank you for helping me bring my animals in for feeding."*

When all of the animals are in for feeding, go back and review what the animals are eating. At this time you can also mention that some animals eat more than one type of food, but it is Farmer Parsons who decides what the animals should eat each day. He wants to keep his animals healthy.

ANIMALS

Make

Chicken - Eggs
Sheep - Wool
Cow - Milk
Pig - Ham
Peacock - Feathers
Turkey - Turkey meat
Goat - Cheese
Barn

Animal products: On one side of the board put the animals. On the other side put a product that we get from each of the animals. First name all of the animals and the products. Go back and point to one of the animals, say the cow, and ask *"What does the cow give us?"* Have a child come up and take the product (milk) off of the board. Then give the cow to another child. Continue until you have mentioned all of the animals and their products.

Put the barn on the board. Say *"All of the animals need to come in for the night. Whoever has the _____ bring it to the barn. Who has the product which the _____ gives us?* Have that child bring that up and give it to you. Continue until all of the animals are bedded down for the evening and all of their products are collected.

Make

Brown bear
Redbird
Yellow duck
Blue horse
Green frog
Purple cat
White dog
Black sheep
Goldfish
Teacher
Children

Brown bear, brown bear, what do you see: Read this story by Bill Martin to the children. After you have read it several times, put the animal characters on the board. Read the story again, but this time let the children guess which animal is next before you turn the page. Have a child come up to the board and point to the animal that has just been guessed before you turn the page. *"Did they guess right?"* Have the first child sit down, finish reading the page, and then have the group guess what animal is next. Have another child come up and point to it. Continue until you have finished the story.

Props

A copy of the book BROWN BEAR, BROWN BEAR, WHAT DO YOU SEE, by Bill Martin

Rex

106

Sort the animals

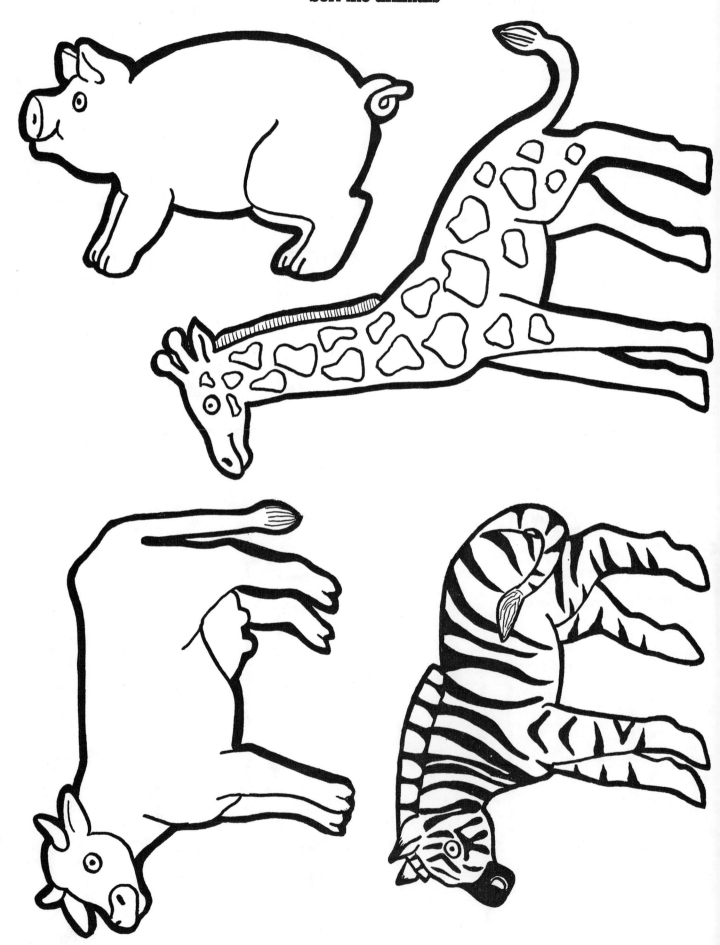

Sort the animals

Animal escape

Animal escape

Feeding time

Feeding time

Animal products

WOOL

MILK

Animal products

Note: Matching animals in previous activities

114

Brown bear, brown bear, what do you see

116

SHAPES

Make

A variety of sizes (same color) of squares, circles, triangles, and rectangles

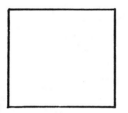

Make

Use appropriate patterns from other activities

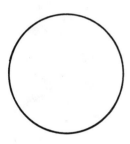

Make

Five felt circles, squares, triangles, and rectangles. They should be the same color but graduated sizes.

Props

Matching posterboard shapes

A square has 4 sides: Pass out all of the square pieces. Ask the children who are holding a felt shape to show it to the others. Have someone quietly call out the name of the shape s/he sees. Then have those who are holding a square, trace around the edges of the shape with their pointer finger. At the same time have the children who are not holding a square make that shape in the air.

Once again have the children with shapes hold them up. Say, *"Billy, put your _____ on the felt board." "Alice put your _____ on the board."* Continue on until all of the squares have been placed on the board.

Pass out another shape to different children. Have them hold their shape high in the air. Continue the activity as explained above.

Name that shape: Put a series of shapes in a row on the felt board. Going left to right, point to each one and have the children call out the names of the shape. Then pose these problems:
***What shape is last? First?
***What is the name of the second shape? Third shape? Etc.
***Name a shape that is red. Blue. Green. Etc.
***"*Sam come up to the board and point to all of the squares — circles — rectangles — triangles."*

Once you have talked about the series and the different shapes, pass out matching shapes to the children. Point to the first shape in the series. Say, *"Whoever has a felt piece which is the exact shape, size and color as this one, bring it up and put it underneath."* Continue through the entire series. When finished, count the different sets of matching pieces.

Match the shapes: Put the felt shapes on the board. Point to each one and name the shape. Pass out the posterboard shapes to the children. Have a child come up and match his/her posterboard shape to the felt shapes. When s/he thinks it is a match s/he turns to the group. If they agree that it is a match, they quietly call out *"Yes"*. If they do not think it is a match, they call out *"Try again"*.

SHAPES

Make

Different size squares, triangles, and circles out of individual pieces of felt

Keep the piece of felt from which each shape was cut.

Fill the space: Pass the individual solid shapes out to the children. Put one silhouette on the felt board. Have the children look at the silhouette and then at their shape. Have the child who has the shape which fits into the silhouette come and put it into the empty space. If it fits, s/he should leave it in the space. If it does not fit, s/he should take it back with him/her and let other children try their shapes until the silhouette is filled. Then put another silhouette on the felt board. Once again have the children look at their shapes and see if they have one which fits into the empty space. Continue until all of the children have found the silhouette which matches their shape.

Make

2 sets of a variety of colored squares

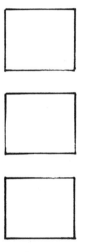

Sequencing squares: Using one set of colored squares, make a simple pattern on the board. For example blue, white, red — blue, white, red — blue, white, red. Point to each square on the board and have the children call out the color. As they are calling out the colors try to get a rhythm going to help them remember the pattern more easily. Then cover up the original pattern. Pass out the duplicate set of squares to the children. Ask them, *"What color was the first square?* (Answer) *If you have that color square hold it up in the air".* Have one of the children bring his/her square up and put it under the first square in the original series. This square will be the first one in a new series. Then ask the children, *"What color was the second square?"* (Answer) *If you have that color hold it up high so I can see it."* Have a child bring up his/her square and put it next to the first one. Continue in this maner until all the children think they have duplicated the original series of squares. Uncover the original series and see if the two series match.

   Mix up the squares into a different series and play again. You can add more squares to the series or change the shapes to make the activity more difficult.

Make

Square, triangle, and circle which fit together to make a bird house

Bird

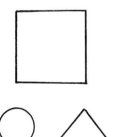

Looking for home: Randomly put the pieces for the birdhouse on the felt board. Point to each piece and have the children call out its shape. Tell the children a short story about a bird who is looking for a house.

   "It was a windy fall afternoon. The trees were swaying, leaves were floating to the ground, and kites were whipping around the sky. A bird was having a very difficult time flying through the air since it was so windy. The more tired he got the more he thought he should look for a place to land and rest. He thought about a tree branch, but that would still be in the wind. He thought about the grass, but then he could not see what was going on. He decided that he needed to find a birdhouse in someone's yard. So he began to look for a birdhouse as he flew around."

   Have the children see if they can help this tired bird by arranging the shapes on the felt board into a birdhouse. After the children make the birdhouse, have the bird fly into it.

SHAPES

Make

Basic shape of a
- Boat
- Car
- Airplane
- Train
- Bus

Variety of small shapes to complete the design of each vehicle

Props

A model of each vehicle

Shapes on the go: Have all of the basic transportation shapes in front of you. Put the small shapes along the top of the felt board. Point to each one and have the children name it. Put one of the vehicles in the center of the felt board. Ask the children what form of transportation the shape reminds them of. Now have the children use the smaller shapes to fill in the detail on the vehicle. For example they can use circles for wheels, squares for windows, rectangles for doors and stairs, etc. Encourage them to 'build in' as much detail as they can. If they need help, have a model to match each felt piece. By looking at the model they will see the detail rather than having to imagine it.

When they have completed their felt vehicle say to a child, *"Randy, please bring me all of the circles we used to build the car."* Continue until all of the shapes are off of the car. Have the last child bring you the basic car shape. Begin again with another vehicle.

Looking for home

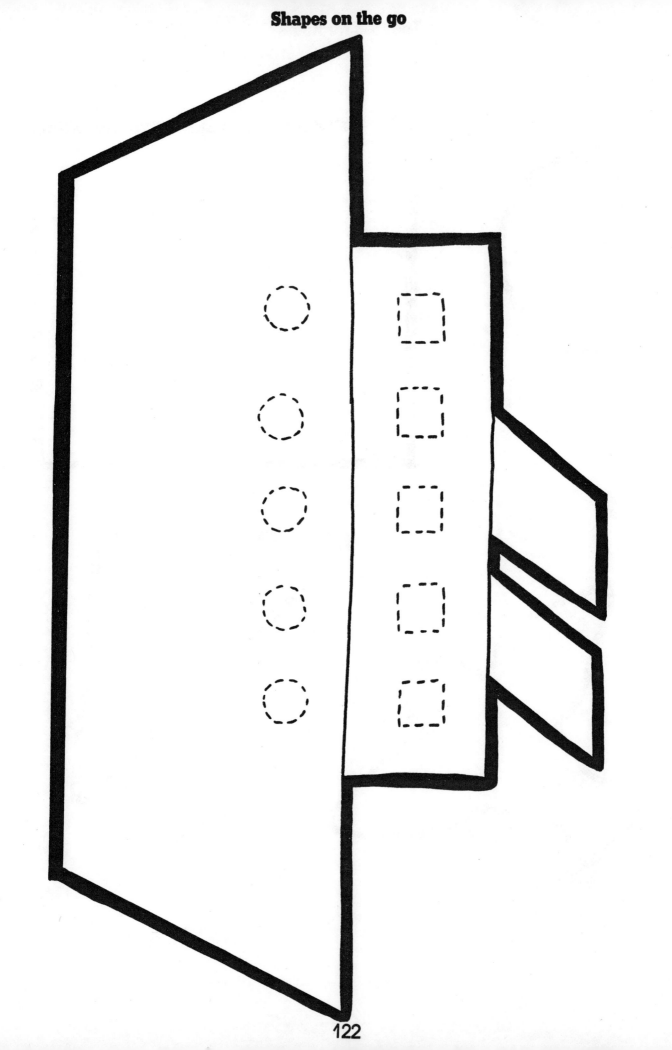

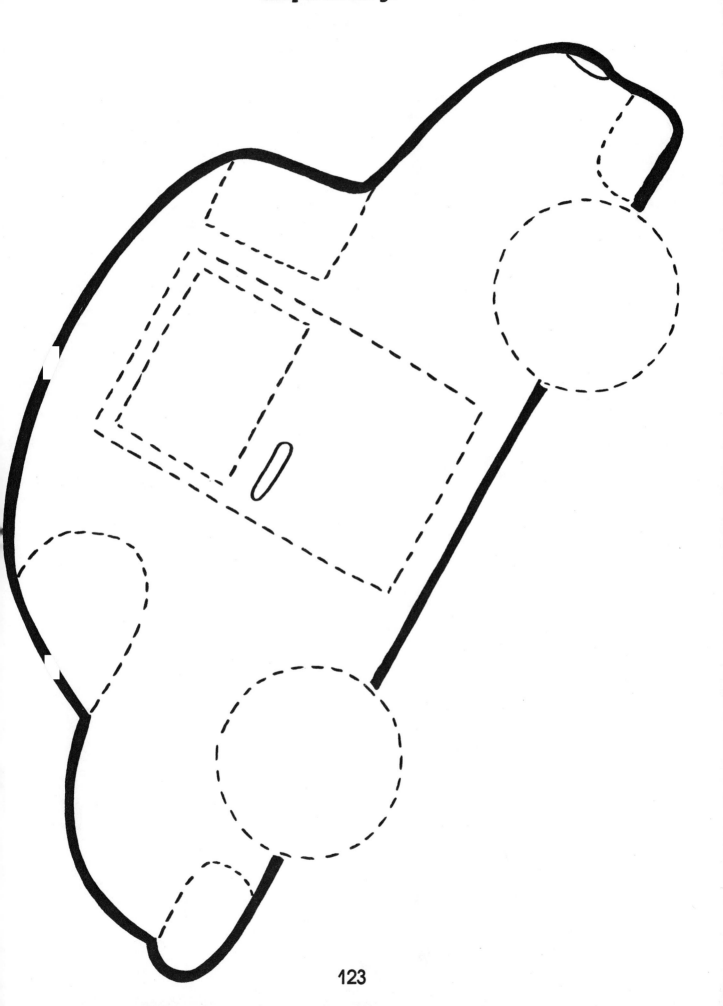

123

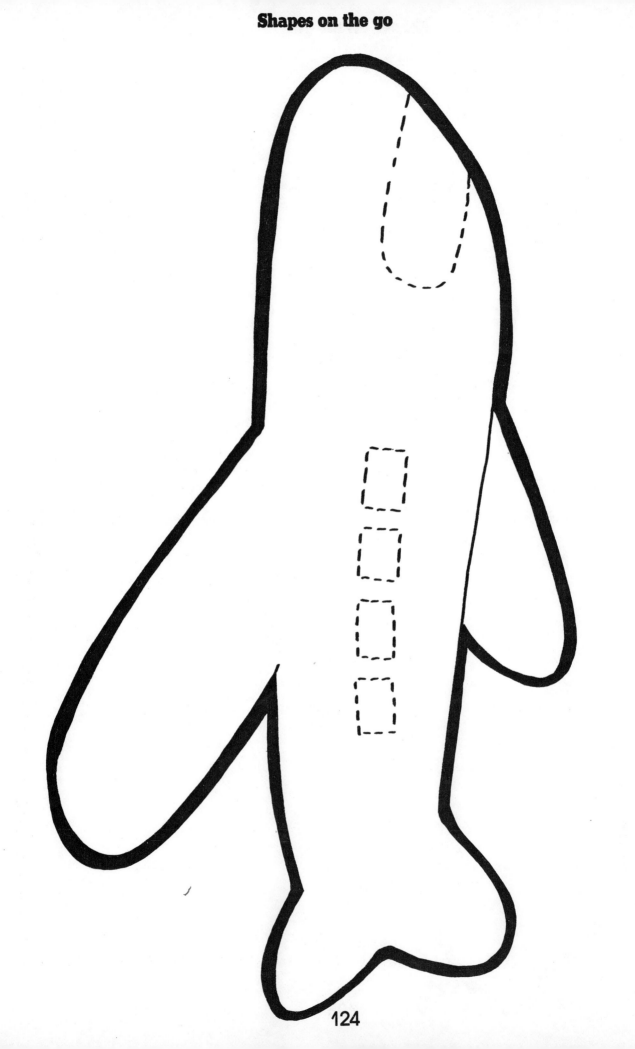

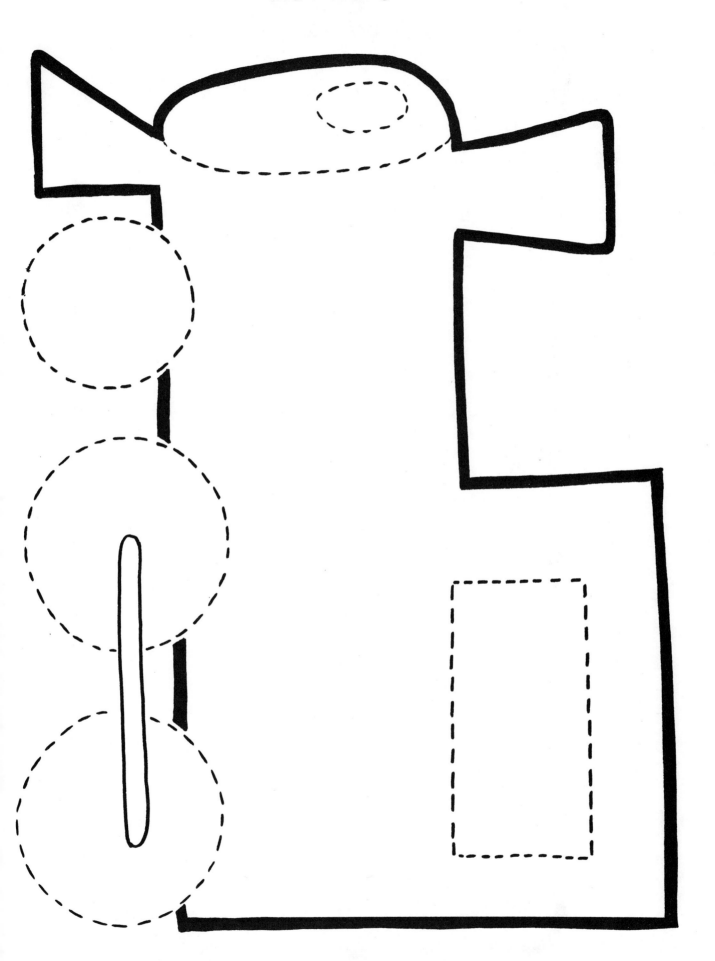

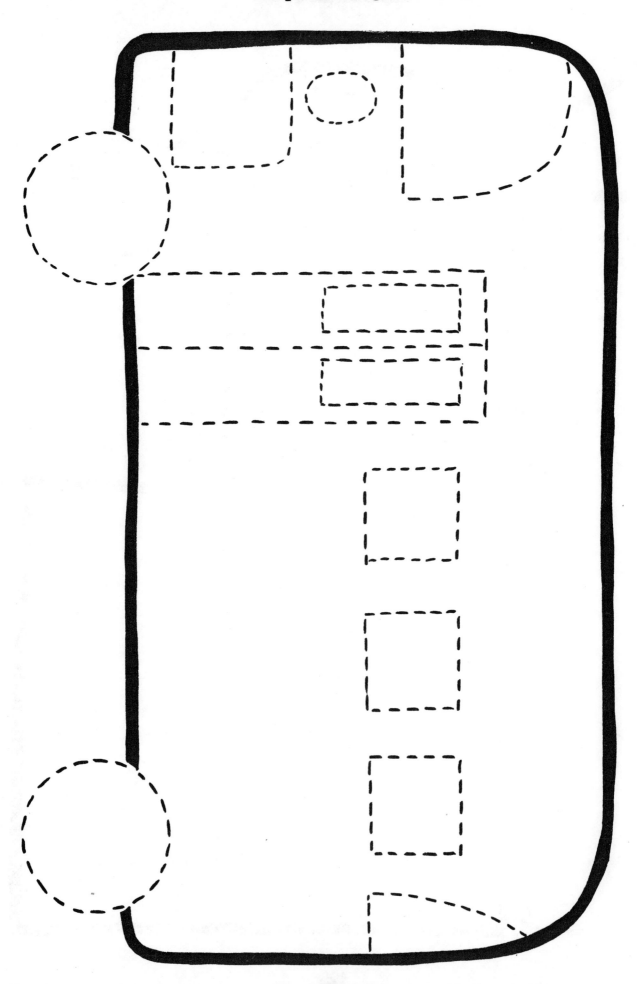

126

COLORS

Make

A matching felt triangle for each color on the spinner board

Props

A large spinner board with the 8 basic colors on it

Spinner fun: Lay the spinner board in the middle of the group. Put the eight colored triangles on the felt board. Have a child go to the center and flick the spinner on the game. When the spinner stops, the group should call out the name of the color to which it is pointing. Then have a child come up to the felt board and point to the triangle which matches the color on the spinner board.

Make

3" circle of each of the the 8 basic colors

Props

A paper plate and 1 set of 8 colored circles about 1" in diameter for each child

Sequencing colors: Put the eight colored circles on the felt board. Point to each one and have the children call out the name of the color word. Then take them off of the board. Give each child a paper plate and a set of circles. Have each child put the circles in a row above his/her plate. Now they're ready to play.

Have the children cover their eyes. While they are covered, you put four or five circles on the felt board. Have them open their eyes and look at your circles. Point to each one and have them call out the color word. Then have them copy your pattern by putting their circles on the plate. When finished the children can point to their circles and call out the colors together. Have them take their colors off of their plates while you take your sequence off of the board. Now play again!

Make

Letter carrier with a large pack
Houses for each color you want to highlight
Several envelopes to match each house

I'm a letter carrier: Put the letter carrier and the houses on the felt board. The letter carrier has a lot of envelopes to deliver and needs some help if all of the people are going to get their mail. Distribute the envelopes to the children and ask them to help the letter carrier. Point to one of the houses. Ask the children what color it is. After they answer, have all of the children with that color envelope pretend to be letter carriers and deliver the mail to that home by putting the envelopes near the house. Continue in this fashion until all of the letters have been delivered.

COLORS

Make

Balloon man with balloons of each color you are discussing — more than one of each color depending on the number of children in your group.

Props

Matching yarn for the balloon strings

Mr. Puffin: Put the balloon man with his balloons on the felt board. Have the children pretend that they have just walked into a circus and the balloon man is at the door. Of course each child wants a balloon to hold and play with during the circus.

The balloon man has so many different colors that it will be hard for each child to choose a balloon. To help each child decide which balloon s/he should 'buy', play this game:

Have each child look at what s/he is wearing, then pick one of the colors from his/her clothing. Once each child has picked a color have him/her come up to Mr. Puffin and say something like, *"I'm wearing a **red** shirt and I would like a **red** balloon to match my shirt."* Then the child should pick a red balloon and take it back to his/her place in the group. When each of the children has a balloon, go around and have him/her tell what color balloon s/he has.

Then have everyone holding 'red' balloons, march up to the front of the group and give you his/her balloon — Children holding 'blue' balloons, hop to the front — Those with 'green' ones, skip — Everyone with 'yellow' ones, twirl — Continue until you have all of the balloons back.

Make

One crayon of each of the basic colors

Props

At least one crayon to match each of the felt crayons
A box for the real crayons

Color crayons: Put all of the felt crayons on the board. Play a variety of games:

***Point to each crayon and have the children call out the color name.

***Say a color name and have a child come up and point to the appropriate crayon.

***Say a color name and have a child come and take that crayon off of the board and keep it. When all of the crayons have been removed say, *"Whoever has the **blue** crayon put it back on the board."* Continue until all of the crayons are back on the board.

***Put all of the crayons in a straight row. Say, *"Jason, tell us the color of the second crayon."* Continue by asking about all of the colors.

***Give each child a real crayon which matches a crayon on the felt board. Point to a felt crayon and say, *"If you have a real crayon which matches the one I'm pointing to, bring it here and put it in this box."* Continue until all of the crayons are back in the box.

Make

Colored paint swatches backed with felt

Light colors-dark colors: Put the variations of the different colors in separate piles in front of you. Take one set of colors. Put the swatches in random order on the felt board. Have the children look at all of the color variations. Then have them find the darkest one and then the lightest one. Once they can distinguish these two extremes have them sort the colors into a series from darkest to lightest and then from lightest to darkest.

Enjoy the activity again using a different set of color variations. If you are talking about a distinct color each day this is a good activity to use at the beginning or end of the discussion.

128

Make

Variety of ice cream cones — at least one for each child.

    Vanilla - white
    Chocolate - brown
    Strawberry - pink
    Licorice - black
    Lemon - yellow
    Orange - orange
    Lime - green
    Grape - purple
    Raspberry - red

Favorite flavors: One of the most exciting things to do on a warm afternoon or evening is to visit an ice cream shop and buy a big ice cream cone. Talk with the children about the different flavors they like to eat. See if they have ever ordered a flavor they did not enjoy. What was it?

Once you've talked about the children's experiences at the ice cream shop, put the ice cream cones on the board. Pretend that you are all going to the local shop to buy an ice cream cone. First have the group get up and walk around the room several times as if they are on their way to the ice cream shop. Then come back to the group area and line up in front of the felt board to order an ice cream cone from you, the clerk. Have each child tell you what 'flavor' s/he would like. Once s/he has placed his/her order have him/her point to the 'flavor', take it off of the board, go sit down, and then pretend to eat the ice cream cone. Once everyone has been served, talk about the taste of the ice cream.

Make

One paint brush of each of the colors you are discussing - at least one for each child in your group
One matching paint can for each of the paint brushes

Props

Box of empty paint cans
A copy of the book, OH! WERE THEY EVER HAPPY, by Peter Spier

Paint the house: Put the paint cans on the felt board. Read the story OH! WERE THEY EVER HAPPY by Peter Spier. As you are reading, talk about the colors that the children in the story are using to paint their house.

After the story, pass out paint brushes to each child. Let the children pretend they are the children in the story. Talk about the colors they would like to paint their own house. As a color is mentioned, have the child who is holding that color brush come up to the felt board and get the matching paint can. Pretend to paint the house. When the paint can is empty, 'throw' it and the brush away.

Make

Full length pictures of people in brightly colored clothes. Back each with felt.

Colorful clothes: Put all of the people on the board. Say a color. Have the children look at the pictures and find the different articles of clothing which are the specified color. Continue in this manner for several colors. Then vary the way you ask the questions to get the children more involved with the specific characters:

    "Jamie, what color is the girl's skirt?"
    "Sam, tell us what colors are in the boy's shirt."
    "Jon, come up and point to the boy's socks. Ask a friend what color they are."
    "The girl is wearing something red. Ian, come up and show us one thing that is red."

COLORS

Props

Pieces of yarn about 12 inches long - one for each child in the group. Vary the colors depending on the ones you are emphasizing

Make

A 'stop and go' light

Yarn bracelets: Stretch each color of yarn onto the board. Point to each piece of yarn and have the children call out the color. Then say each child's name and tell him/her what color of yarn to take off of the board. *"Melinda, come and get this 'black' piece of yarn."* When Melinda gets the 'black' piece of yarn, have her give it to you. You tie the piece of yarn around her wrist. Continue until each child has a piece of yarn tied around his/her wrist. Throughout the day talk with each child about his/her special color. When the children go home, have them tell their parents about the color. Have them try to wear something the next day that is the same color as their piece of yarn.

Stop and go: Put the 'stop and go' light on the board. Point to each color. Have the children name the color and discuss what it means. Now play an exercise game using the light. First demonstrate an exercise, such as clapping your hands. Tell the children that when you point to the green light they should begin to clap. When you point to the yellow light they should slow down and when you point to the red they should stop. At this point you can demonstrate another exercise and repeat the activity with the new exercise or you can point to the yellow light again which would mean the children should get ready to clap and then when you point to green they can clap again. Continue with a variety of exercises.

I'm a letter carrier

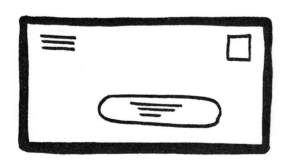 

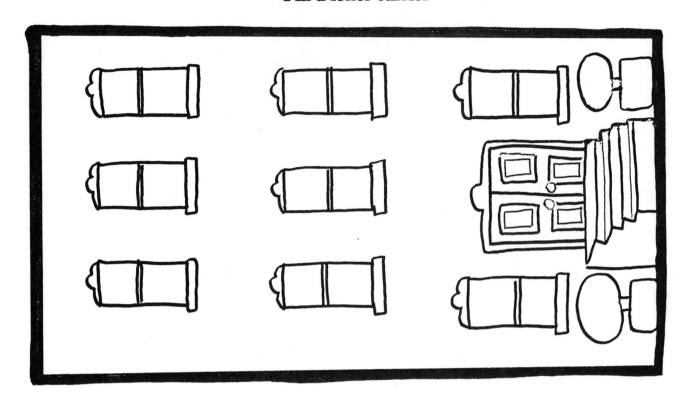

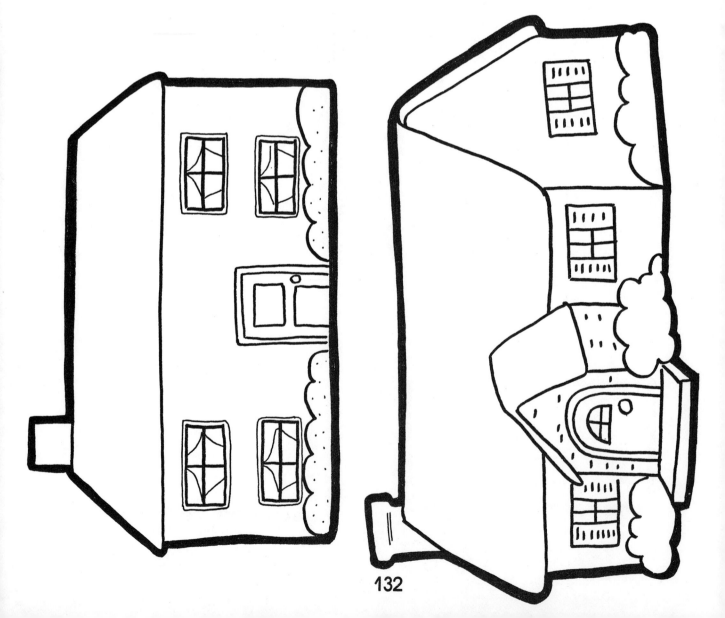

Mr. Puffin

Color crayons

Favorite flavors

134

Paint the house

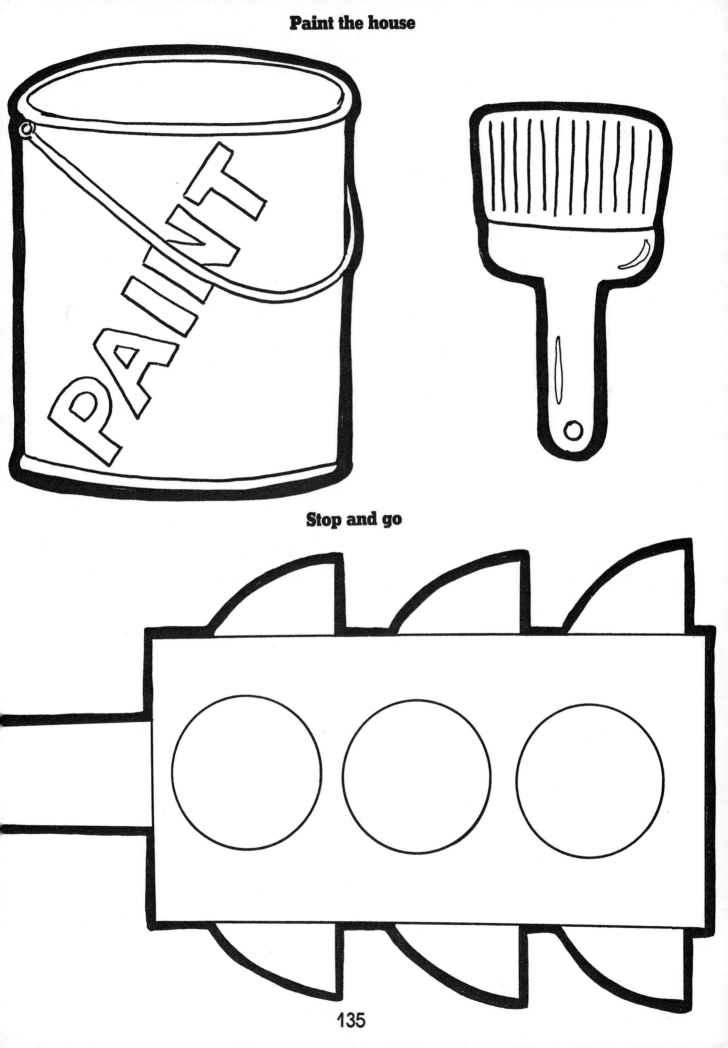

PAINT

Stop and go

Make

Upper and lower case letters

Naming your letters: Separate the letters into two piles — upper case and lower case. Put the two piles in front of you. Using one pile at a time, put one letter in the center of the felt board. Have the children call out the name of the letter. Move that letter off to the side of the board. Put another letter in the middle of the board. Have the children name that one. Continue until all of the letters are named.

On another day repeat the activity with the other set of letters.

Make

Upper and lower case letters from the activity NAMING *YOUR LETTERS*

Who has the letter: Pass out either the upper or lower case letters to the children. Ask, *"Who has an 'H'? Put it on the felt board."* When all of the letters are on the board put them in order with the children. Say, *"I'm looking for the 'A'."* Have one of the children come up, find it, and then put it in the beginning of what will eventually be an alphabetical listing of the letters. Continue throughout the entire alphabet. When all of the letters are in order, sing an alphabet song. Point to each letter as you sing.

Make

Upper and lower case letters from the activity NAMING YOUR LETTERS

Alphabetizing: Separate the upper and lower case letters into two piles. Take one pile and spread the letters out in the middle of the circle so all of the children can see them. Then say, *"I'm looking for the letter 'A'.* The child who finds it can put it in the upper left hand section of the felt board. Continue alphabetizing by asking for the 'B' 'C' and so on to 'Z'.

On another day play the game with the other set of letters.

Make

2 or 3 sets of upper and lower case letters that are made from 5 or 6 colors of felt

Name that letter: Pass out the upper case letters. Say to the group of children. *"Whoever has a **red** letter put it on the felt board."* When all of the 'red' letters are on the board, point to each one and have the group call out the name of the letter. When the group has identified the last 'red' letter, take the letters off of the board. Then say, *"Whoever has a **blue** letter put it up on the felt board."* Once again identify each letter. Continue until the group has named all of the upper case letters.

Play this game another day using the lower case letters.

ALPHABET

Make

Upper and lower case
letters from the
activity NAMING
YOUR LETTERS

Props

Set of upper and lower
case alphabet cards

Matching letters: Put the upper case (or lower case) letters in order on the board. Have a set of matching alphabet cards. Hold up a card. Have the children name the letter and then look for the matching felt letter. When a child finds it, have him/her go up and get it. Continue until the children have all of the felt letters. Call out the names of all of the letters. As you call each letter, have the child holding that letter bring it up. When all of the letters have been returned sing the alphabet song.

Make

Upper and lower case
letters from the
activity NAMING
YOUR LETTERS

Props

Magazine and
newspaper
advertisements with
large letters

Using letters: Put the advertising pieces in front of you. Pass out upper and lower case felt letters which match the letters in the advertising copy. Hold up one of the advertising pieces. Read what the ad says and talk about the product. Then point to one of the letters in the ad. Say, *"I'm pointing to an upper case M. Who has the M? Put it on the felt board."* Continue with the rest of the letters in that ad and then go to the next advertisement.

Make

Upper and lower case
letters from the
activity NAMING
YOUR LETTERS

Matching upper and lower case letters: Put the upper case letters on the felt board leaving space for the lower case letters in between. Pass out the lower case letters to the children. Point to one of the upper case letters, for example 'F' and say to the children, *"I'm pointing to the upper case F. Who has the matching lower case f.* The child who has the 'f' should put it next to the 'F'.

Make

Upper case letters from
the activity
NAMING YOUR
LETTERS

Props

Namecards for each
child

Your name's important: Put all of the upper case letters on the felt board. Hold up each child's namecard. When the child recognizes his/her name, have him/her come up and get the card. When everyone has a card, you're ready to begin the activity.

Have a child stand and hold up his/her namecard, say his/her name and tell the other children what the first letter in his/her name is. For example, *"My name is Heather and it begins with an H.* Then that child chooses another child and says, *"Peter, go to the felt board and point to an H."* Peter does this. When Peter comes back to his place, have him hold up his namecard and continue the activity.

ALPHABET

Make

Stop sign
Yield sign
Speed Limit 25 sign
Caution sign
School Crossing sign
Merge sign

Make

Shopping cart
Brown grocery bag
Corn
Milk
Bananas
Potatoes
Soap
Juice
Ham
Noodles

Props

A boldly written
shopping list with
each of the above
items on it

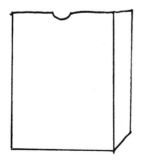

Letter walk: Enjoy this story with the children.

"It was about time for the parents to pick up their children from school. The day was so beautiful that Jimmy's and Adrienne's mothers walked to school to get them. Jimmy's mom had a great idea for a game on the way home. Because Jimmy and Adrienne were learning to recognize and name letters, they would look for signs as they walked home. When they saw one they would stop and Jimmy and Adrienne would 'read' as many of the letters on the sign as they could recognize. They all started walking towards their homes looking for signs. 'There's one' said Jimmy. (Put the STOP sign on the board. Say to the children, "Let's help Jimmy 'read' the letter on the sign." Point to each letter and have the children call out the letters they recognize.) *On they went after 'reading' the letters on the STOP sign. Adrienne's mom saw the next sign. She asked Adrienne to 'read' the letters on the sign.* (Put the YIELD sign on the board and let the children 'read' the letters.) *Adrienne and Jimmy were really enjoying this game.*

Continue the LETTER WALK until Jimmy and Adrienne have noticed all of the signs and named the letters.

Trip to the grocery store: Take an imaginary trip to the grocery store. Begin by saying, *"You and your dad are going to help the family by going to the grocery store. Your mom has written a list of all of the things that she needs.* (Point to each word on the list as you read it to the children.) *Now you're ready to go. The store is only several blocks away so you and your dad decide to walk. Soon you're there. You get your cart* (Put it on the board.) *and take out the list your mom gave you. There are eight things you need to buy.* (Put all of the items off to one side of the board.) *You begin by going to the vegetable section of the store. There are two vegetables on your list.* (Ask the children what they are. Have a child come up and point to one of the felt vegetables. 'Read' each letter written on that food. Then have the child put it in the cart. Repeat the activity with the second vegetable.) *The fruits are near the vegetables. Mom has one of the family's favorite fruits - bananas - on the list. She said that she would make a banana salad for dinner tonight."* (Have a child come up and point to the bananas. Have the child 'read' each letter and then put the bananas in the cart.)

Continue telling the story and having the children 'read' each letter on every product that John and his dad are buying. When all of the items are in the shopping basket, put the large brown bag on the felt board. *"It is time for you and your dad to check out. As the clerk checks out each food, the bagger at the store puts it into a large bag."* (Say each item. As you do, have a child put that item in the bag. Before you leave, check each item against the grocery list to see if you have bought everything that mom needed.)

Q R
S T
U

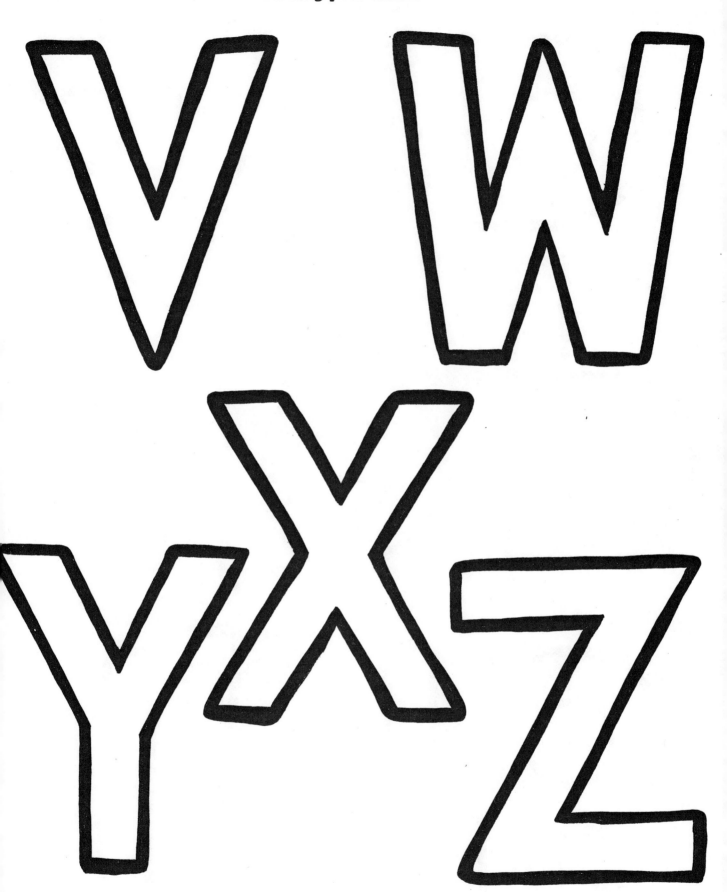

a b c
d e f
g h i j

k m n
l o p q
r s t u

V W X

Y Z

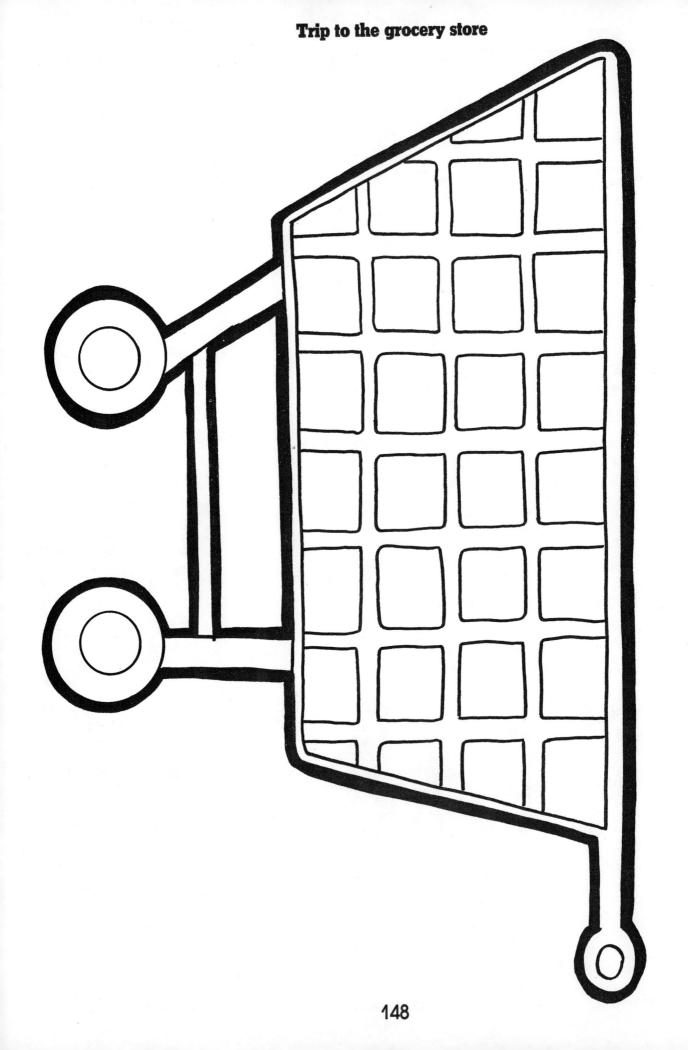

NUMBERS

Make

Numerals from 1-10

Counting: Put the numerals from 1-10 on the felt board. Beginning with the number 'one' point to the numerals and count. Let your voice get softer and softer as you say each number. When your voice is barely audible, ask the children which number you said last. They can take their cues from two sources since they were listening to you and they can see which numeral you are pointing to on the felt board.

Make

Use the 1-10 numerals from the activity COUNTING

Number rhymes: Put the numerals from 1-10 on the felt board. Enjoy your favorite number rhymes with the children. As the group is saying the rhyme, you point to the appropriate numeral on the felt board.

Here are a few number rhymes with which to begin:

I CAN EVEN COUNT SOME MORE
One, two, three, four
I can even count some more.
Five, six, seven, eight,
All my fingers stand up straight.
Nine, ten are my thumb men.
ONE, TWO, BUCKLE MY SHOE
One, two buckle my shoe,
Three, four shut the door,
Five, six pick up sticks,
Seven, eight lay them straight,
Nine, ten a big fat hen.
ONE, TWO, THREE
One, two, three! There's a bug on me.
Where did he go? I don't know.

Make

Birthday cake
10 candles
Use the 1-10 numerals from the activity COUNTING

Happy Birthday: Put the birthday cake without candles on the felt board. Have the ten candles off to the side. Have one of the children come up to the board. Say to that child, "*I have a friend who's name is Sam. He is going to be 4 years old on his birthday. Erin, please put 4 candles on Sam's birthday cake.*" (Let Erin do this. As she is doing it, have the group count the candles. As Erin is walking back to her place, take the 4 candles off of the cake and continue the activity.) "*Sam has an older sister who just had a birthday. She was 8 years old. Peggy, please come up and put 8 candles on her cake.*" (Let Peggy put the candles on the cake as the group counts. Once again take the candles off and continue.) "*When Sam's mother was 10 years old she had a party. At that party her Dad pretended to be a clown. He played lots of funny tricks for her friends. Margie put 10 birthday candles on the cake.*" (Margie puts 10 candles on the cake. The children count as she does it.)

Continue talking about different birthday parties. Have the children put candles on the cake to represent the different ages you are talking about. Conclude the activity by singing *Happy Birthday* to everyone.

VARIATION: In addition to the candles have the appropriate numerals off to the side of the cake. As each child puts the appropriate number of candles on the cake, have him/her also find the matching numeral and put it on the cake.

NUMBERS

Make

Giraffe without spots
10 spots numbered —
1-10 on one side

Make

10 ducks
Pond

Joey gets his spots: Keep the spots in front of you. Put the giraffe on the board. Ask the children to identify the animal. Tell them that his name is Joey and Joey needs something. See if anyone can guess what he needs. Then say, *"You're right, Joey needs his spots. You know, I think Joey left his spots at my house last night. When I went to my car this morning, I found these white spots next to the driver's seat. I didn't know what they were until just now. Let's count as I put them on Joey."* Put the spots on Joey. Let the children count as you put them on.

***Put the spots on the giraffe with the numeral side up. Point to each spot and have the children identify it.

***Put the spots in random order near the top of the board. Have a child find the first spot and put it near the top of Joey's neck. Find the second spot and put it just under the first one. Continue until Joey has all ten of his spots.

Count the ducks: Put ten ducks in a row on the felt board. Have the children count them forward and backward. Remember to touch each duck as the children count or have a child come up and touch each duck as the group counts. If a child does the pointing be sure that s/he touches the ducks in order. You may need to move his/her finger along.

***Put the pond on the felt board. Put a specific number of ducks on the pond. Count them with the children. When you have finished counting say, *"We have 4 ducks on the pond."* Clear the pond. *"Now how many ducks are on the pond?"* The children will say *"None"* or *"Zero"*. Put a different set of ducks on the pond. Repeat the counting activity. Remember to clear the pond before a new set of ducks waddles on.

***Pretend the felt board is the farmyard. Put the 10 ducks in a group in the farmyard. Put the pond off to one side of the farmyard. Tell the children that some of the ducks are going to waddle onto the pond. As you are moving the ducks have the children count them. Ask the children, *"How many ducks went to the pond?"* Let the children answer. Recount if necessary. Then say, *"Let's see how many ducks stayed in the farmyard."* Count those ducks with the children and determine how many were left in the yard. Now have the ducks that were in the pond waddle back to the group. Count the entire group of ducks. Have a different number waddle over to the pond. Count them and then count those which were left in the farmyard. Continue with several more groups of ducks.

NUMBERS

Make

Large blue circle
10 rocketships —
  numbered 1-10
Large yellow circle

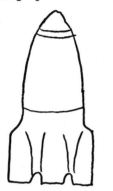

Blast-off: Pretend that the felt board is outer space. Put the moon on the upper part of the board. Put the rocketships in random order on the board. Have one child come up to the board, find Rocketship Number 1, take it off of the board, fly it around the room, and then have it land on the moon. Have another child come up and find Rocketship Number 2. Fly it around the room and have it land on the moon. Continue until the last rocketship has landed.

Put the earth on the board. 'Blast' the rocketships off the moon and give them to different children. When they have all blasted-off, say "*The person with Rocketship Number 1 bring it back to earth.*" Have that child fly the rocketship back to earth. Continue until all of the rocketships have safely landed on earth.

End the activity by saying, "*Because of the long journey each rocketship will need a thorough inspection. They will stay in storage hangers until the next space flight.*"

Make

Apple tree
Five apples
Apple core

Delicious apples: Put the apple tree and five apples hanging from the tree on the board. Tell this number story. As you use a child's name, have him/her come up and take an apple from the tree.

"*There were five big, juicy red apples hanging on the apple tree in the orchard. Julie was running through the orchard on her way to visit a friend. As she passed the tree, she jumped up and picked one. Now there were four apples on the tree. Adam and Larry were also roaming in that orchard. They had been playing tag and were very hungry. When they saw those apples they just had to each have one. They reached up and picked two more. Now there were only two left. Carrie was walking her dog through the orchard. She had not had a snack yet, so she ate one. Now there was one apple left on the tree. Who do you think ate that last apple. (Let the children guess and then say) Before any more children came along, a family of worms crawled out to that last apple and ate most of it up. When the wind came along, the core fell to the ground. (Put the core on the board.) Now there were no apples left on the apple tree in the orchard.*

1234
567
890

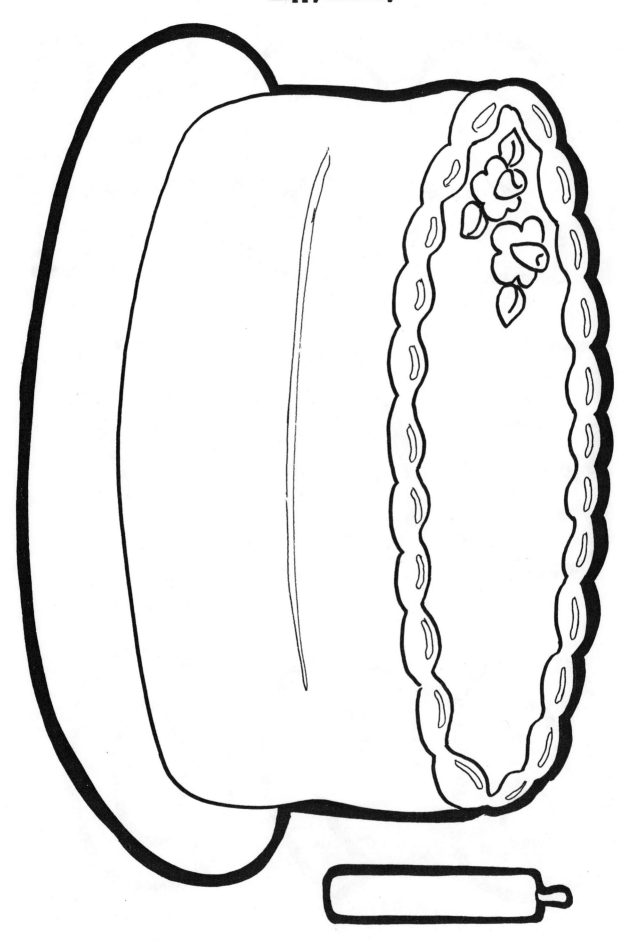

Joey gets his spots

Count the ducks

Blast-off

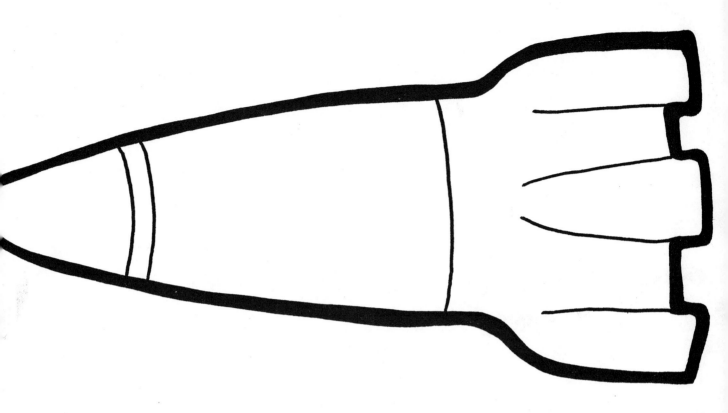

Delicious apples

HOLIDAYS

NEW YEARS DAY

Make

Blowers
Horns
Rattles
Tambourines
Ratchets

Props

Several of each type of noisemaker — at least one for each child

Welcome in the new year: Have the different types of felt noisemakers in front of you. Pass the real noisemakers to the children. First tell all of the children to blow/shake/twist their noisemakers. Next go around the circle and let each person briefly show the others how his/her noisemaker works. Then put one of the felt noisemakers on the board. Have the children look at their noisemaker. If anyone has that type, have him/her hold it up in the air. Once everyone can match his/her noisemaker to a felt board piece, enjoy this activity:

Clear the felt board. Tell the children that while they are closing their eyes, you are going to put one of the felt noisemakers on the board. When they open their eyes they should look at the piece on the felt board. If it is the same as their noisemaker, they should play it until you take the felt noisemaker off of the board. Have them close their eyes again while you put another piece on the board. Continue as above.

VARIATION: Instead of putting the felt noisemakers on the board one at a time, put on two or three each time you change the pieces. Then the children will play 'in concert'. The last time you do this, put all of the felt noisemakers on the board. When the children open their eyes, everyone can WELCOME IN THE NEW YEAR!

Make

Numerals for the year you are currently in and the one you are celebrating — use the numerals from the NUMBER section

It's a new year: Though young children do not understand the concepts of calendars and yearly progression, it is fun to talk about the idea of the past and future. Begin by putting the numerals of the current year on the felt board. Ask the children a variety of questions about things they might have done during the recent past, such as what they received for holiday gifts, what their favorite ways to have fun are, and visiting friends. You might expand this by discussing activities they had done in school during the fall.

Then talk about this holiday as the beginning of a new year. Put the numerals for the new year below those of the current year. Talk about which numerals stayed the same and which one/s changed. The one/s that changed represent/s the new year. Ask the children what they might do during the remainder of the winter. Do any of them have a birthday? How old will they be? At this time you can also mention the word resolution and talk about what it means.

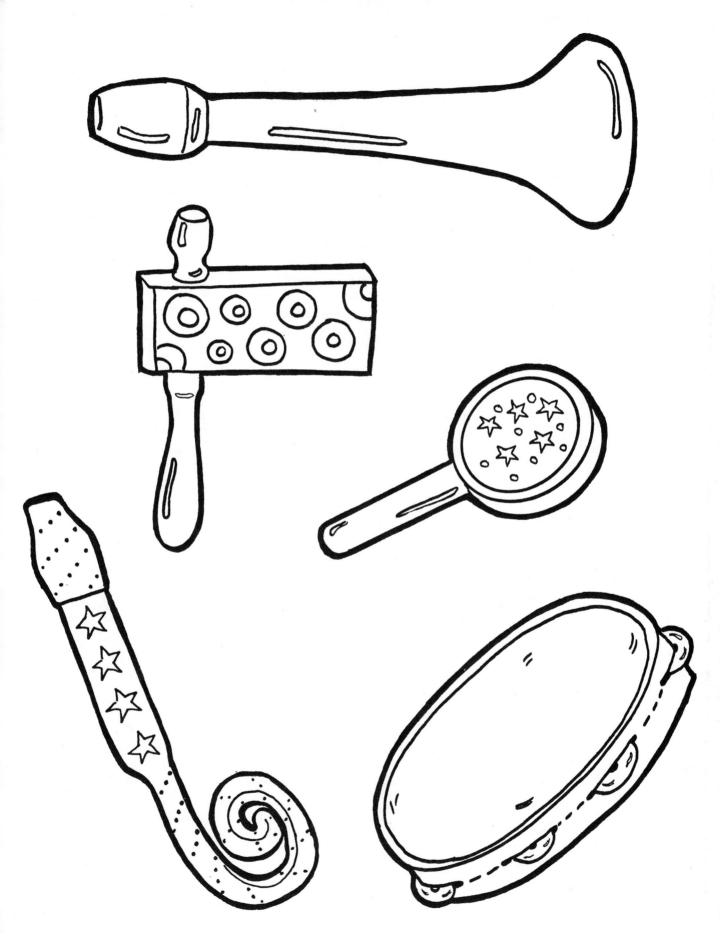

MARTIN LUTHER KING jr.

Make

A star for each child in the group
Large ribbon with 'Nobel Peace Prize' written on it
10 smaller Nobel Peace Prizes

I have a dream: On January 15 the people of the United States celebrate Dr. Martin Luther King, Jr.'s Birthday. He was an American civil rights leader who lived from 1929-1968. Dr. King was a Baptist minister who led the black struggle for equality through non-violent means. His philosophy is best described through his own words from a speech he gave in Washington D.C. on August 28, 1963. "I have a dream that one day this nation will rise up and live out the true meaning of its creed: 'We hold these truths to be self-evident; that all men are created equal.'" Because of his peaceful approach, he was awarded the Nobel Peace Prize in 1964. He was the youngest person ever to win that award.

Talk with the children about the dreams that they have had while sleeping. Let them tell each other about those dreams. Then help them to understand that the type of dream that Martin Luther King, Jr. had was not the type of dream you have while you are sleeping, but was more like a wish or hope for the future. Talk about wishes they have had. Have them pretend that it is their birthday. What do they hope they will get for a present? Then ask them if they have ever had any adult in their family wish for something. What was that wish?

Now that the children have a better understanding of wishing and dreaming, pass out a felt star to each child. Have them each think of one wish they would like to come true. It can be a wish for themselves or a wish for someone else. As each person tells what his/her wish is, have him/her put the star on the felt board.

EXTENSION: Put the 'Nobel Peace Prize' on the board. Talk about disagreements in the classroom and acceptable ways to solve the problems. Then put several of the smaller 'Nobel Peace Prize' ribbons on the board. Tell the children that to celebrate this holiday they should all try to be peacemakers. Whenever someone helps to solve a problem peacefully s/he will wear a 'Nobel Peace Prize'. This can continue throughout a week or so.

Nobel Peace Prize

VALENTINES DAY

Make

A tree with empty
  branches
Small hearts, each with
  a child's name
  written on it

Friendship tree: Put the empty tree on the board. Then begin hanging the hearts on the branches. As you hang each heart, read the child's name which is written on it. When all of the hearts are on the tree, have the children cover their eyes. Rearrange all of the hearts. Then have the children uncover their eyes. One at a time, have a child come up to the tree and find his/her name.

After each child has identified his/her name, pin the felt heart to his/her shirt. Then sing the song about *Valentine Hearts.*

VALENTINE HEARTS
One little, two little, three little hearts,
Four little, five little, six little hearts,
Seven little, eight little, nine little hearts,
Bring love on Valentine's Day.

Make

Between 5 and 10
  graduated hearts
  and arrows

Hearts and arrows: Put the hearts on the board in random order. Decide which one is the largest heart, the smallest one, which ones are in between. Count the hearts. Then add the arrows to the board. Count the arrows. Are there as many arrows as there are hearts? Find the largest arrow and put it with the largest heart. Find the smallest arrow and match it to the smallest heart. Continue matching the hearts and arrows until all of the pairs have been made.

Make

A large red heart
10 white circles about
  1½-2 inches in
  diameter

Count the circles: Put the large Valentine heart in the middle of the felt board and the white circles near the top. Enjoy math games with the circles:
***Count the circles forwards and backwards.
***Put a specific number of circles on the heart. Count them. Take them off. Put a different number of circles on the heart. Count again. Continue with a variety of sets.
***Put all of the circles on the heart. Count them. Have a child come up and take a specific number off of the heart. As the child takes them off, have the group count them. Put the circles back on the heart. Count all of them again and then have another child come up and take a different number off. Continue in this manner.

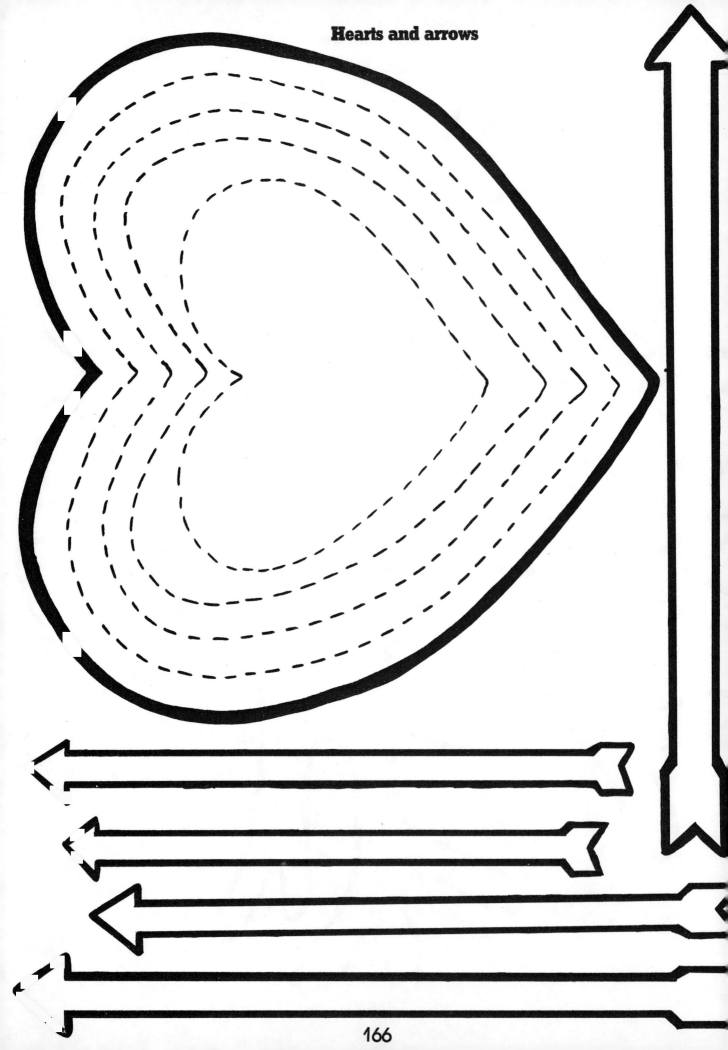

ST. PATRICKS DAY

Make

10 bags of gold with the numerals 1-10 written on them
55 pieces of gold

Bags of gold: Put the bags of gold in order from 1-10 on the felt board. Arrange the pieces of gold near the bottom of the felt board.

Point to each bag and have the children call out the name of the numeral which is written on the bag. When you are sure that your children can recognize the numerals, say, *"Pedro, put three pieces of gold on the bag marked 3."* After he has put a certain amount on the number '3' bag, point to each piece of gold and count them aloud with the children. Continue in this fashion until all of the pieces of gold are safe in the bags.
VARIATION: Turn the bags of gold over so none of the numerals are showing. Put them in a straight row. Say, *"Shawn put two pieces of gold in the second bag."* After he has done this, count the gold pieces with the group. Continue in this manner until all of the bags are filled with gold.

Make

Patrick
1 shamrock for each child

Patrick needs shamrocks: Put Patrick in the middle of the felt board. Pass the shamrocks out to the children. Tell each child where to put his/her shamrock in relation to Patrick. As you give the directions, accent the position words. Here are several with which to begin:
"Betty, put your shamrock on Patrick's hat."
"Matthew, hide your shamrock behind one of Patrick's feet."
"Julie, let Patrick hold your shamrock in one of his hands."
"Dick, put your shamrock near Patrick's coat."
"Carol, put your shamrock under Patrick."
"Paul, Patrick needs a shamrock in his other hand. Put yours there."
"Liz, put your shamrock as far away from Patrick as you can."

Make

3 different size shamrocks. Cut the leaves and stems of each shamrock apart.

Shamrock puzzles: Keep the stems off of the board during the beginning of the activity. Put the leaves of all the shamrocks in random order on the board. The children should look at all of the leaves and decide which ones go together to make shamrocks. Have one child come up to the board and choose three leaves s/he thinks fit together. Have him/her put the leaves together in shamrock form. Continue until all of the leaves have been made into shamrocks. Look at all of the shamrocks. Do any of them need to be rearranged?

Now add the stems. Taking turns, let the children put the appropriate length stems on each of the shamrocks.

Bags of gold

Patrick needs shamrocks

PASSOVER

Make

Sofa
Chair
Lamp
China cabinet
Stool
Table
Rug
Afrikoman

Find the afrikoman: Put the pieces of furniture on the felt board. Tell the children that the Seder leader is ready to hide the afrikoman. Have the children cover their eyes. Put the afrikoman behind one of the pieces of furniture. Have them uncover their eyes. Let a child guess where the afrikoman is hiding. When s/he makes his/her choice, have him/her come up and look behind the piece s/he chose. If the afrikoman is there, have the children cover their eyes and hide it again. If it is not, have another child guess. Continue until it is found. Play several times.
VARIATION: For younger children, who might find it frustrating not to have any clues as to where the afrikoman is, put it in a more visible place. Then have the children be very specific about where it is — *"**Under** the sofa"* OR *"**Between** the table and chair"* OR *"**Over** the stool"* OR *"Laying **in the middle** of the rug"* OR *"**In** the china cabinet"*.
EXTENSION: Enjoy a piece of matzah for snack.

Make

Hard-boiled egg
Lamb bone
Salt water
Greens
Bitter herbs
Haroset
Matzah
Seder plate

Seder food: Several days before the Seder meal, explain the traditional foods to the children. Tell them the meaning of each food as you place it on the felt board.

Now let the children pretend that they are helping their family prepare for the Seder meal by gathering the food which goes on the special plate. Put the plate on the felt board. Their dad says, *"Put the food on the Seder plate which symbolizes the strength of the Jewish people.* (Have a child put the hard-boiled egg on the plate.) *Find the bread which is baked without yeast or salt.* (Have another child find the matzah and put it in the center of the Seder plate.) Continue until all of the foods are on the Seder plate.

Take this opportunity to let the children tell each other how they will celebrate Passover. Talk about preparations for the Seder meal including the thorough house cleaning, use of special china and tableware, who they might visit, and so on.

Find the afrikoman

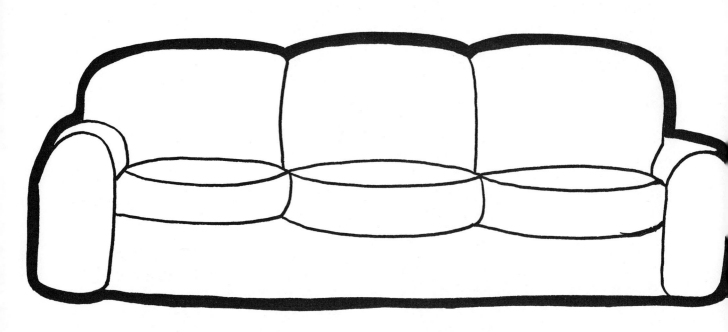

Find the afrikoman

APRIL FOOLS DAY

Make

Use the numbers in the
NUMBERS section

April Fool's Day: Play a variety of felt board activities which
will try to 'trick' the children.
***Put the numerals in order from 1-10 on the board.
Reverse two numerals. Your row might look like
1,2,3,4,5,7,6,8,9,10. Have a child come up to the board
and point to each numeral as you count. See if the
children can discover where the 'trick' is. When they do,
have the child put the numerals in the correct order.
Have the children cover their eyes. Reverse two different
numerals. When the children uncover their eyes, count
again. Continue several more times.

What's missing pieces

Cat without a tail -
cat's tail
Airplane without a
wing - wing
Car without a tire -
tire
Table without a leg -
leg
Hot air balloon without
a basket - basket
Coat without buttons -
buttons
Stop sign without
letters - S T O P

***Keep the 'what's missing' pieces in front of you. Put the
first one on the board. Have the children identify
who/what the piece is and then tell what part of the
piece is missing. When they have identified the missing
part, put that part in the appropriate place. Continue
with all of the other 'trick' pieces.

What's wrong pieces

Carpenter hammering
a clothespin
Monkey eating a
baseball
Truck with square tires
Drum major carrying a
hockey stick
Dog playing the piano
Whale with an
umbrella
Firefighter with a
sprinkling can

***Have the 'what's wrong' felt pieces in front of you. Put the
first one on the board. Let the children look at the piece
and decide what is wrong. When someone knows s/he
can tell the others. Then have the children create other
ways to make the felt piece silly. For example, ask the
children, *"What other silly things could the carpenter be
hammering?"* After they have named some, then ask
"What does a carpenter really hammer?" Continue with
the other pieces.

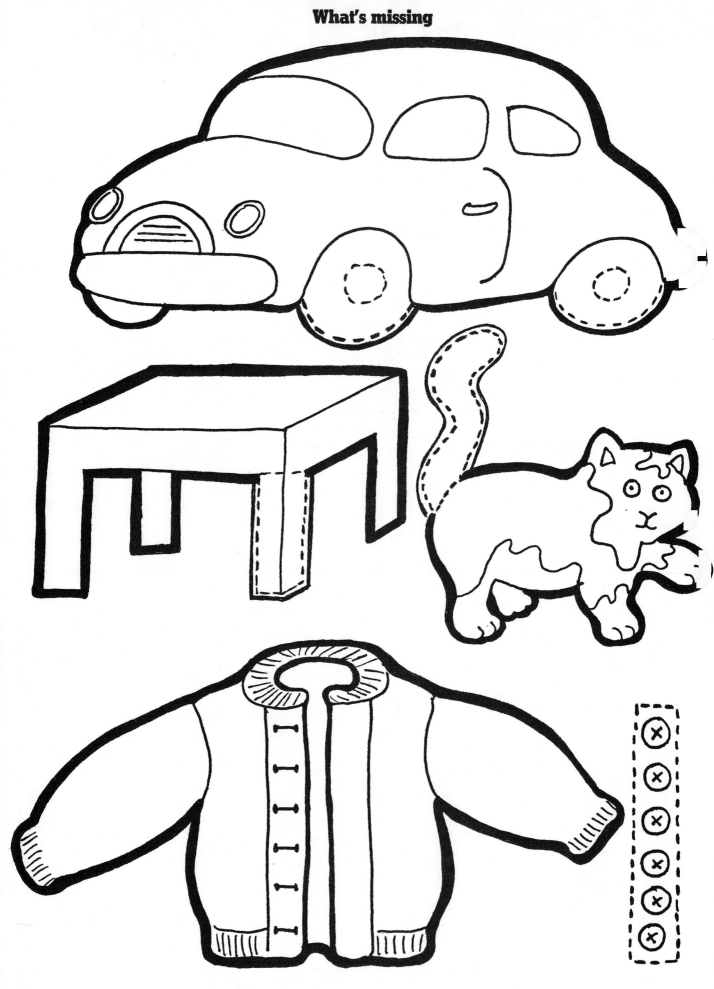

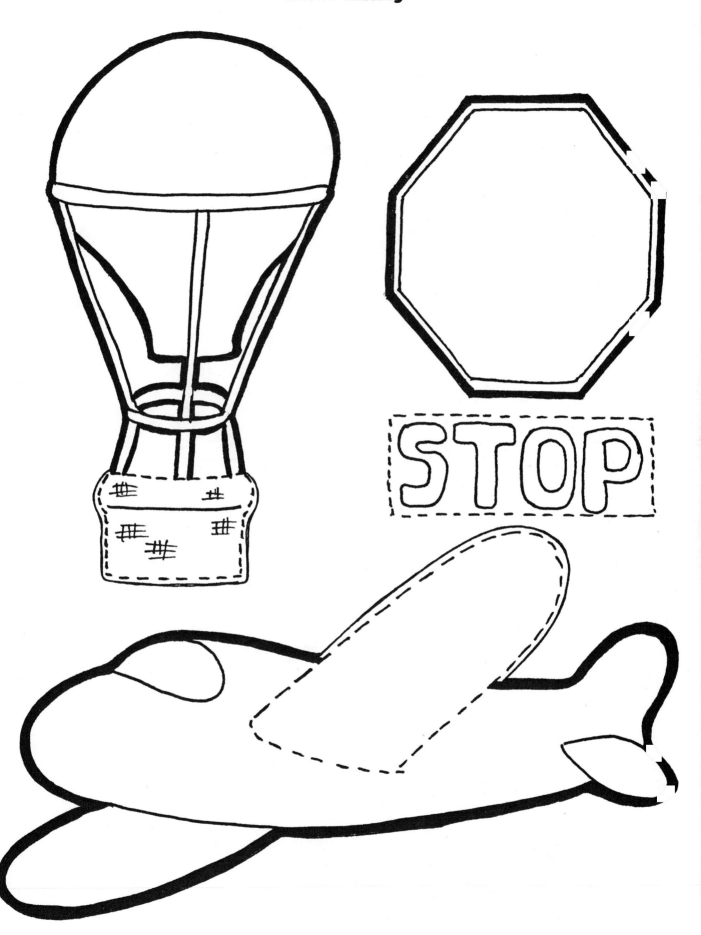

STOP

EASTER

Make

Empty - Full Easter
  basket
Baby chick - Adult
Baby rabbit - Adult
Plain hard boiled egg -
  Decorated egg
Sugar - Candy rabbit
Undecorated hat -
  Frilly hat

Easter fun: Talk about all of the things you do to get ready for Easter. Down the left side of the felt board put the felt pieces which show the first stage of each Easter symbol. Put the other pieces in a random group on the right side of the board. Start with the first symbol - the empty basket. Talk about what happens to the empty basket. Then have the children find the completed Easter basket and put it next to the empty one. Proceed to the next symbol. Talk about it and then find its mate. Continue talking about and matching symbols.

VARIATION: To make this activity more difficult have more than two pieces in the series for each symbol, for example an empty basket, one with Easter grass in it, and then the completed one.

Make

Four sets of differently
  decorated eggs

Props

One small Easter
  basket for each
  child
One basket for the
  teacher

Easter egg match: Before you play this game with the children, put one complete set of eggs in your basket. Fill each of the children's baskets with several felt eggs.

To begin the game give an Easter basket to each of your children. Let the children examine their eggs. Put one of your eggs on the board. Have the children look through their baskets again and see if they have an egg which matches the one you put on the board. If they have one, let them come up to the felt board and put it near the first egg. Continue until all of the eggs in your basket are matched with all of the eggs in the children's baskets.

Make

A different chick for
  each child in the
  group
A duplicate set for the
  teacher

Cheep-cheep-cheep: Give each child in the group an Easter chick. Put one of your chicks on the felt board. Have the children look at their chicks. If someone thinks that s/he has a match, let him/her bring it up and put it next to the teacher's chick. Let the other children look at the chicks. If they match have the children excitedly say, *"Cheep! Cheep! Cheep!"* If it is not a match, the child should take his/her chick back and continue to watch for a match. After the first chick is matched, put another chick on the board and continue.

When all of the chicks are matched you should have the same number of chick pairs as you do children in your group. Count each and see if the number is the same.

Easter egg match

Cheep-cheep-cheep

183

Make

Drum
Silhouette of a house.
 Cut flaps for doors in
 each room

The lost drum: Before doing the activity with the children, put the drum on the felt board and the house over the drum so that it is hidden behind one of the doors. Bring the board when you are going to play the game.

Parades are a favorite way to celebrate this summer holiday. Billy was going to be a drummer in his town parade. He could not wait. Enjoy this story with the children:

"It was the morning of the Fourth of July and Billy was very excited. That afternoon he is going to play his drum in the town parade. He ate breakfast with his family and then went to get his drum from the closet. Oh no, the drum wasn't there! (Bring out the felt board with the silhouette of Billy's house on it. Tell the children they will have to help Billy find his drum.)

Billy knew that the drum was someplace in his house, but he could not remember where he had put it. He went back to the kitchen and asked his mom if she had seen it. She said, 'No.' His dad suggested that he look in every closet in the house. Billy thought that was a good idea."

Ask the children, *"Which room do you think Billy should begin in?"* Whatever room they suggest, open the door and see if the drum is in it. Continue opening doors until someone finds Billy's drum.

EXTENSION: Have the children pretend they are Billy marching in the town parade with his drum.

Make

White rectangle about
 18" by 12"
7 red stripes, 4 short
 and 3 long
Several white stars
Blue square 6" by 6"

Props

A small United States
 flag for each child

Make a flag: Because the children will see many flags for this holiday, it is an appropriate time to talk about the flag. Pass out a flag to each child. First talk about the colors they see in the flag. Then count the white stripes — the red stripes. What color stripe is on the top of the flag? On the bottom? What else is on the flag? Tell the children there are fifty stars in all. When you have finished discussing the flag, have them carefully lay it on their lap.

Put the large white rectangle on the felt board. Place the blue square in the upper left-hand corner of the flag. Ask the children what goes on the blue field. *"Stars."* Pass out the stars you have made. Have the children put the stars on the blue field one at a time. As they put the stars on the flag, have everyone else count. When finished, remind them that in a real flag there are fifty stars, but yours has only

_____ stars. Then pass out the seven red stripes. Remind the children that the red stripe was at the top. Have a child come up and lay a short red stripe across the top of the flag. Continue laying the red stripes across the flag until it is finished.

The lost drum

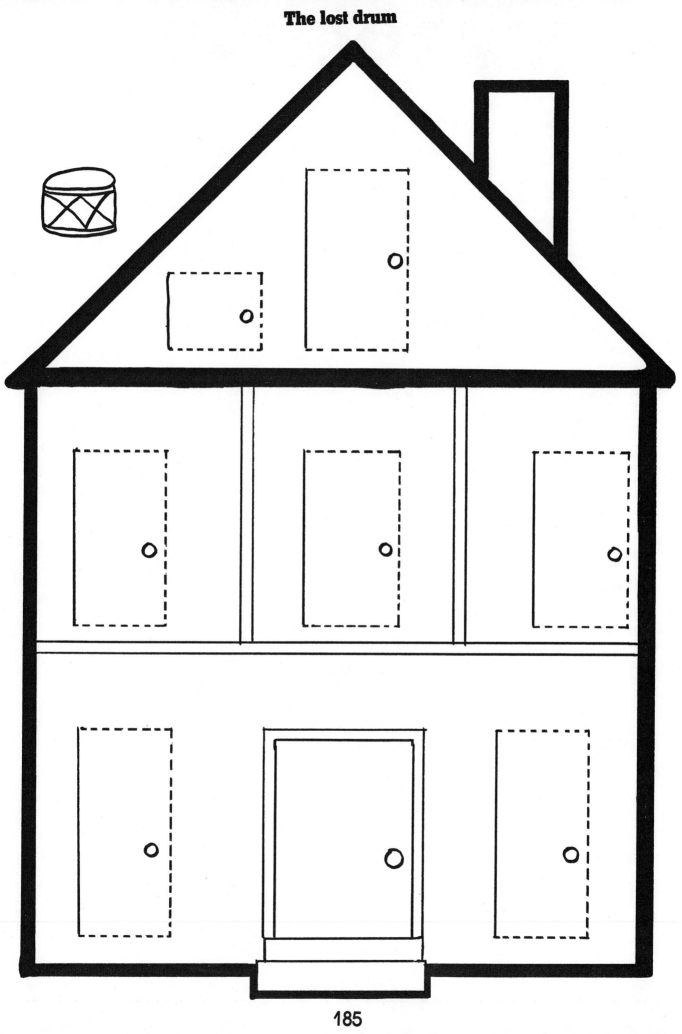

LABOR DAY

Make

Construction hat
Letter carrier hat
Police officer hat
Nurse cap
Baker/chef hat
Butcher hat
Firefighter helmet
Pilot hat
Football helmet

Whose hat: Put all of the hats on the board. Ask the children, *"Do any of you know someone who wears these hats?"*
Depending on the answers, continue to talk about the people who wear them. Include the reason why people wear special hats and what jobs they do.
EXTENSION: Let the children choose from several different hats and make one at art time. They can wear them throughout the day and pretend to be a certain type of worker.

Make

Hammer
Letter cart
Hand cuffs
Stethoscope
Mixing spoon
Knife
Hose
Compass
Football

Props

Have a real tool to
   match each of the
   felt tools

Name that tool: People use a variety of tools to perform their jobs. Have the real tools in a box in front of you and the matching felt tools within easy reach. Pass out the real tools so each child gets one. Go around the circle and have each child name his/her tool and show how it works. Then have him/her put the tool down so everyone can see it.

   Put one felt tool on the board. Have the class call out its name. Then have everyone look around and figure out who has the matching real tool. As each child discovers who has the real tool, have him/her point to the child. When everyone is pointing to the child say, *"Emil has the hammer."* Put another felt tool on the board and once again figure out who has the matching real tool.

   When all of the tools are on the board, go back to the first one. Point to it and say, *"This is the felt hammer. Whoever has the real hammer bring it up here and put it back in the box."* Continue until all of the tools are in the box.

Make

Use the hats and tools
   from WHOSE HAT
   and NAME THAT
   TOOL

Props

Pieces of yarn about
   two feet long

Workers and tools: Put the felt hats down the left side of the board and the tools down the right side. Pass out the pieces of yarn. Ask a child who does not have a piece of yarn to tell the others which worker would match which tool and then call on a friend who has a piece of yarn to match them by connecting the hat and the tool with the piece of yarn.

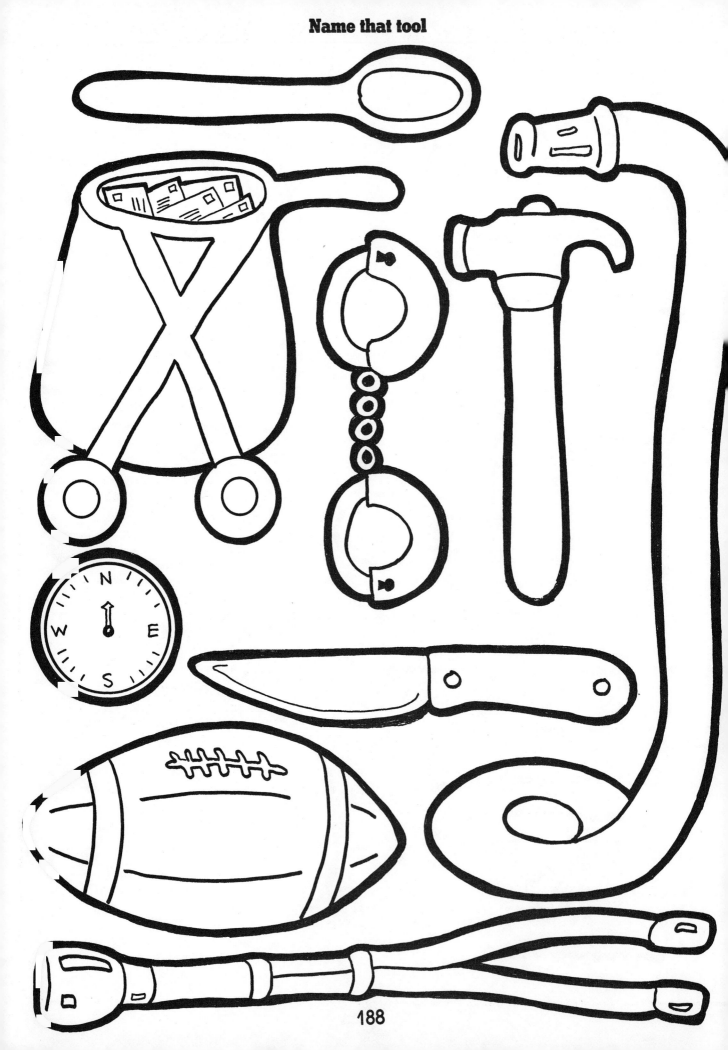

COLUMBUS DAY

Make

3 ships
Whale
Ocean fish
Seagulls
Tropical land

Props

A telescope made out of paper towel roll for each child

Sailing, sailing: Pretend that the felt board is the ocean. Have all of the felt pieces in front of you. Using the felt pieces, tell the story of how Christopher Columbus and his crew discovered America in 1492.

Begin the story by putting the three ships on the felt board. Discuss how Columbus gathered a crew and supplies. Ask the children what they think the sailors ate while they were on the ships. Pretend to load these foods on board. After this discussion, set sail for America and continue the story using the felt pieces. As you add a piece talk about life on the ships. It was a very long voyage and the sailors saw many things. Enjoy discussing whales and the variety of other ocean creatures. Talk about how the sailors caught fish to eat for their daily meals. Encourage the children to figure out what jobs the sailors did to maintain the ships and themselves — cooking, putting up and taking down the sails, scrubbing the ships, reading maps, caring for the sick, etc. What did the sailors do for fun?

Just before you add the 'seagull' and the 'lush tropical land' give the children telescopes. Have them pretend they are sailors. They are all tired and discouraged. They have been looking for land for so many days now. Many of them are angry at Columbus, however they keep looking. All of a sudden one of them begins to shout. *"I see sea gulls!! Land must be near!"* All of the sailors looked through their telescopes. (Have the children look at the felt board through their telescopes. As they do add the 'land'.) When they have the land in sight, have them shout out *"I SEE LAND!!!"*

Columbus and his crew were so excited. They had finally reached land. They rowed up to the shore. As they got to the land they put the flag of Spain in the ground.

After relating the story, talk about how the sailors felt when they finally saw land. Encourage the children to once again pretend to be sailors. Ask them how they felt as they got off of the ship. What do your children think was the first thing the sailors did as they were standing on land?

Dolphin

Sailing, sailing

Shark

Swordfish

Skate

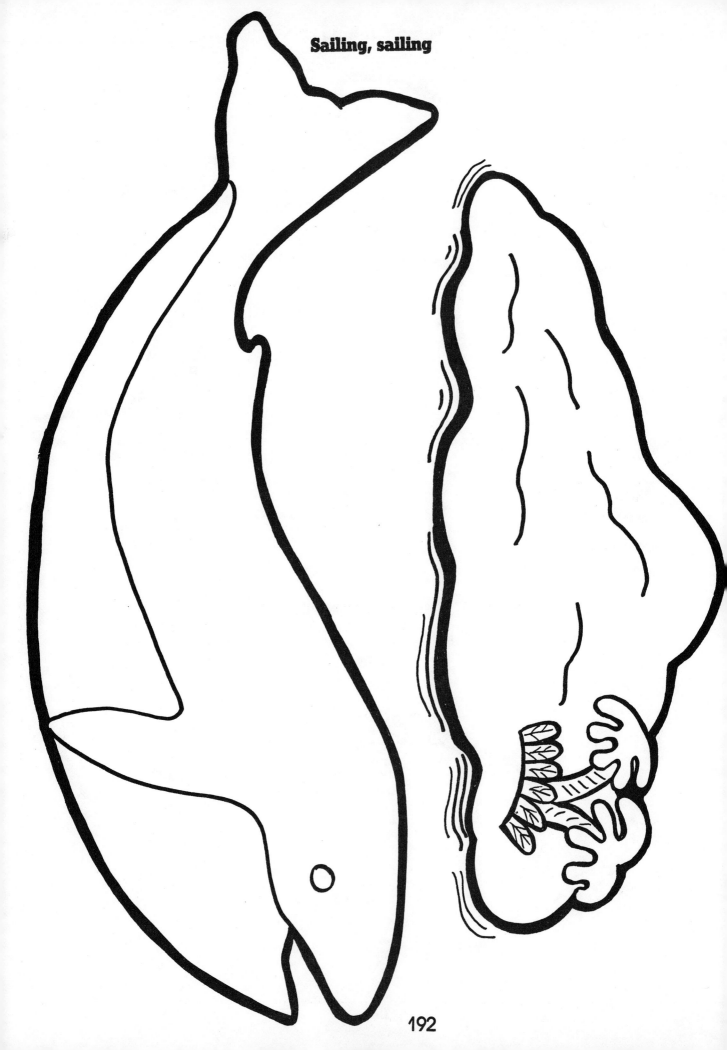

HALLOWEEN

Make

Monster
Cat
Bat
Ghost
Skeleton
Pumpkin
Scarecrow
Witch

Halloween night: First put all of the Halloween characters near the bottom of the felt board. Point to each one and identify it. Now use the characters to compose a Halloween song to the tune of 'The Farmer in the Dell' with the children. Begin the song

HALLOWEEN NIGHT

The witch is in the yard, the witch is in the yard, (Put the witch near the top of the board.)
Hi, ho, its Halloween, the witch is in the yard!
The witch takes a monster (Put the monster next to the witch.)
(Continue the song using all but one of the characters.)
The _____ stands alone, the _____ stands alone (Put the lone character in the middle of the board.)
Hi, ho, its Halloween! The _____ stands alone!

Make

Crown
Witch hat
Ghost face
Clown hat
Cat face
Scarecrow straw hat

Guess who I am: Tell this story before your Halloween party:
    "*It is the day before our school Halloween party. I know that you are very excited and looking forward to seeing each other dressed in different clothes. One of the games we are going to play at the party tommorow is 'Guess Who I Am'. Today we are going to play this game with felt characters so we will be all set to play it with each other.* (Put the crown on the felt board.) *'I came to the party in a beautiful coach. I always wear this crown so people know who I am. Can you guess who I am?'* (Let the children guess all of the different characters who might wear a crown. Also ask the children if any of them are going to wear a crown to the party. Put the witch hat on the board and continue the story in a crackling voice.) *'Sometimes people are afraid of me. That's because my nose is usually very long. Who am I?'* " (Have the children guess who this character is. You can also have the children close their eyes and try to picture what else the witch might be wearing. Then put the ghost face on the board and continue the story as above, letting the children guess who the character might be. Add the remaining pieces one at a time until all of the characters are at the party.)

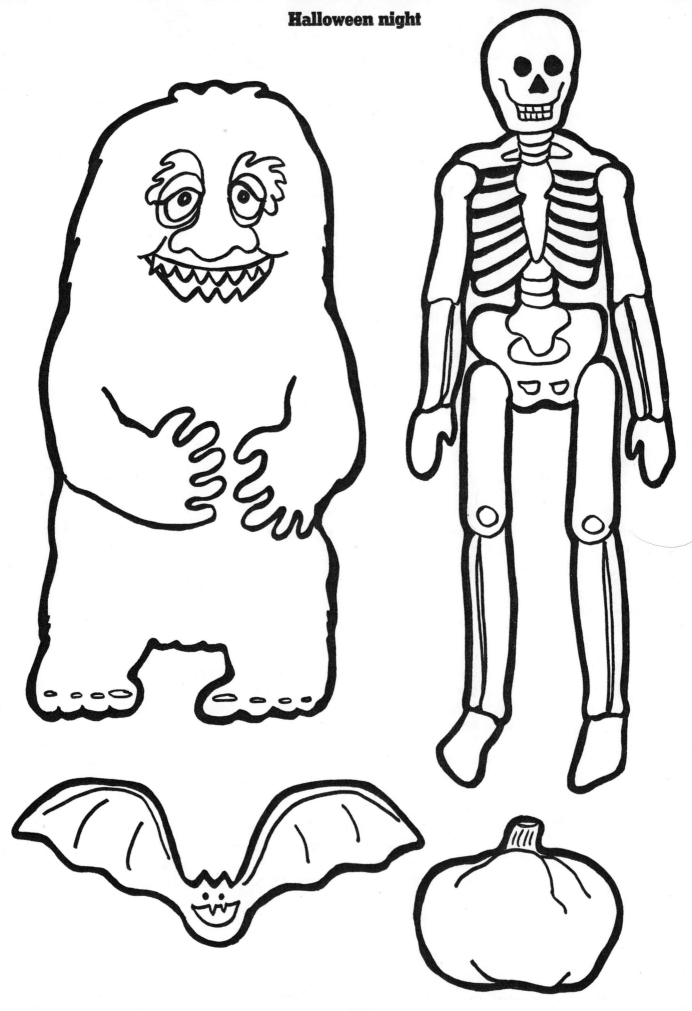

THANKSGIVING

Make

Cornucopia
Apple
Pear
Banana
Strawberry
Orange
Carrot
Potato
Onion
Lettuce
And others

Horn of plenty: Put the empty cornucopia on the felt board. Have the fruits and vegetables in two piles in front of you. Put the fruits, one at a time on the cornucopia. Have the children identify each piece as you put it on. Then put the vegetables on the cornucopia, identifying each one of them. When the cornucopia is full, talk about which fruits and vegetables the children like and do not like.

Make

Turkey body
Different colored
   feathers for each
   child

Thanksgiving turkey: Put the turkey body on the board. Pass out the colored feathers to the children. Have each child come up to the board, tell the others what color feather s/he is holding and then add it to the turkey's tail. When the turkey has his full plumage of feathers, point to each one, and have the children call out the color.

Make

Turkey on a platter
Stuffing
Cranberry sauce
Potatoes
Rolls
Corn on the cob
Jello
Butter
Salt and pepper
Milk
Pie
Ice cream
Plates
Several 1" by 2" strips
   of white paper
   backed with felt

Thanksgiving feast: Thanksgiving dinner is a special event in many United States families. Create a Thanksgiving meal with the children. Begin by discussing the children's plans for the day. Which children will be going to visit friends and relatives? Will there be other children at the Thanksgiving feast? Who? What games will they play? What will the adults do at the party?

  After you've discussed who will be at the feast and what the children will do, begin planning the meal. Pretend that your felt board is the table where the family will be eating the meal. First set the table. Talk about everything you would need on the table. Though you'll discuss all of the necessary items, you'll probably only have room for the plates. Pretend the other objects are there. Then talk about the foods. As a child relates a food s/he might have, put it on the table. (If a child mentions a food for which you don't have a felt piece, write the name of the food on one of the white strips and put it on the Thanksgiving table.)

  After the meal is all planned, go back and talk about the foods. See if there are one or two foods that everyone likes. What are they?

  Pretend to eat the Thanksgiving feast. When you are all finished, name each food that you ate. As you name a food have a child come up to the board, find the food, and give you the piece.

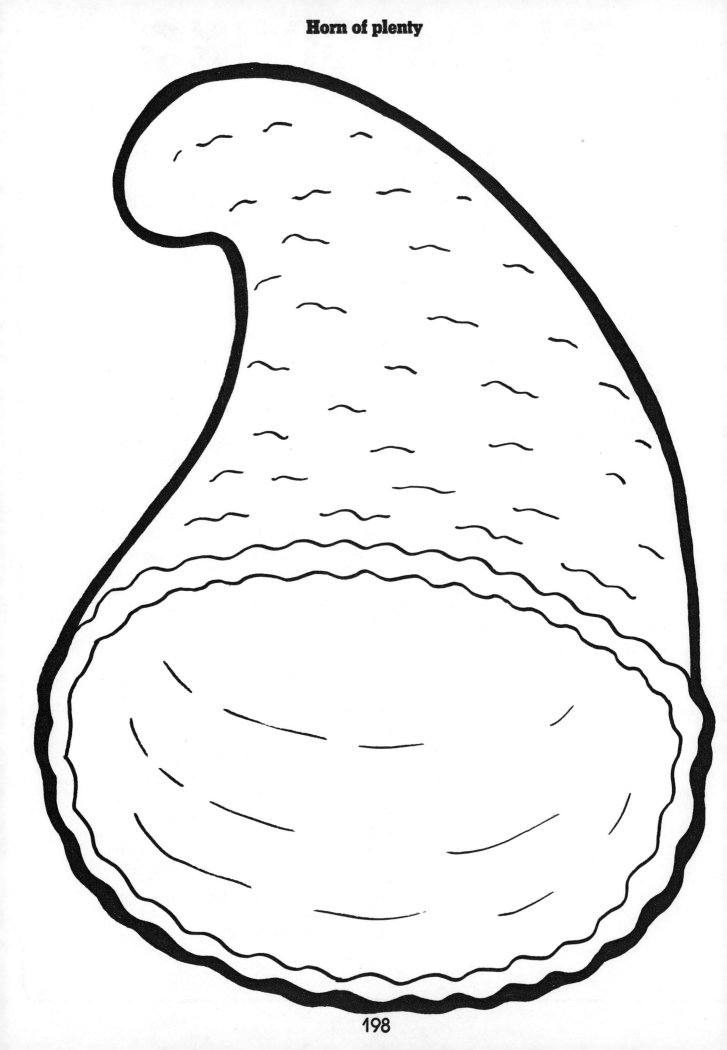

ST. NICHOLAS DAY

Make

Large door
Ten pairs of shoes

Shoe scramble: Begin this activity by saying, *"It's December 5th and the children and parents are just about ready to go to bed. Before they do, however, they need to find their pairs of shoes and put them outside the bedroom door. When they go in their closet they find all of their shoes have been mixed up. The children and adults need some help getting ready for St. Nicholas."*

Put the shoes on the felt board in random order. Have children take turns finding matching shoes and taking them back to their space. When all of the shoes have been paired, put the door on the felt board. Now say, *"Whoever has shoes that a baby would wear, put them outside the door. (Do it.) Whoever has shoes a dad would wear, put them outside the door. (Do it.) Who has tennis shoes? Bring them up here for St. Nick to fill."* (Continue until all of the shoes are ready for St. Nick's visit.)

Talk about what small gifts would be appropriate for the people who wear each type of shoe.

Make

A 4" shoe for each
child in your group
with his/her name on
it
A bag large enough to
cover all of the gifts
One gift for each child
in your group plus
several more:
   Orange
   Crayons
   Ball
   Car
   Doll
   Blocks
   Paints
   Book
   Markers
   Socks
   Barrette
Use the door from the
   activity SHOE
SCRAMBLE

St. Nick's bag: Before you do this activity, put all of the gifts together on the left side of the felt board. Put St. Nick's bag over the gifts so they are hidden. When the children have gathered, bring out the felt board.

Give each child the shoe with his/her name on it. Say to the children, *"St. Nick's pack is filled with treats for all of you. We're going to take a peek and see what is in there."* Now put the door on the right side of the board. Continue the activity by having a child bring his/her shoe up to the board and put it near the door. Then say to the child, *"St. Nick is going to leave you a gift from his pack, but you'll have to help him. I'm going to loosen the top of the pack and you pull out the gift that is on top."* (Pull the top of the bag gently away from the board so the child can take a gift.)

When the child has a gift, have him/her put it in his/her shoe and tell the others what St. Nick left. Let each child grab a gift from St. Nick's sack and put it in his/her shoe. When everyone has a gift, go back and point to each shoe and say, *"St. Nick left Romona a/n _____."* All of the children call out the name of the gift. Repeat this with everyone's gift.

Shoe scramble

St. Nick's bag

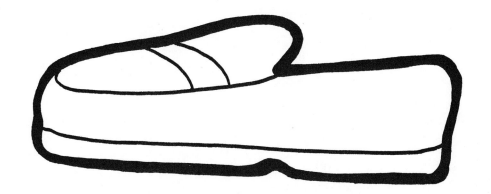

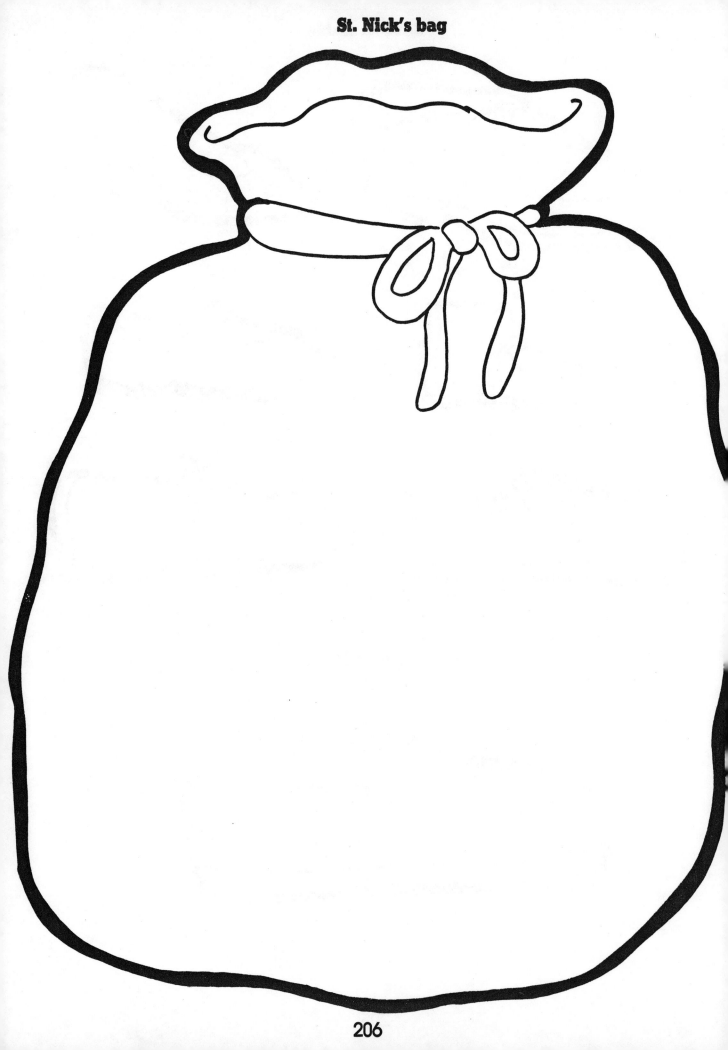

HANUKKAH

Make

Two identical sets of:
- Candle box
- Star of David
- Dreidel
- Menorah
- Candles
- Latkes
- Elephant
- Coins
- Jug of oil

Props

Pieces of yarn

Hanukkah symbols: Put one set of Hanukkah symbols down the left side of the felt board. Point to each one and have the children name it. Then put the matching set in a different order down the right side of the felt board. Ask one of the children to name the first symbol. Then have another child come up, take a piece of yarn from in front of the board, and connect the symbols which match. Continue until all of the symbols are matched. Play again.

Make

Each side of a Dreidel
- 'Nun' player gets nothing
- 'Gimmel' player wins all
- 'Hay' wins half the pot
- 'Shin' adds one piece to the pot

Props

A Dreidel
At least one nut per child

Dreidel fun: Put the four sides of the dreidel on the felt board. Name each side and tell the children what each sign means. Then have a child spin the real dreidel. Ask the children the name of the symbol which is facing up. Now have a child come up and point to the matching felt piece. Continue until all of the children have had an opportunity to spin the dreidel.

EXTENSION: Give each child a nut. Have them put their nut into the middle of the circle. Each time a child spins the dreidel, figure out what move the player would make if s/he were playing "Gimmel Takes All".

Make

Use the pieces from the activity HANUKKAH SYMBOLS

Props

A large piece of posterboard divided into 9 equal sections Draw a simple picture of each Hanukkah symbol to match the felt pieces. Write the numerals 1-9 in the boxes

Hanukkah match: Put the gameboard in the middle of the group so all of the children can see the symbols. Point to each one and have the group identify it. Then put the felt symbols on the board and name each one.

Have a child go to the gameboard, point to a symbol and say to a friend, *"David go to the felt board, find the other dreidel, and put it on the gameboard."* After David matches the dreidels, he points to another symbol, and says to a friend, *"Aaron, go to the felt board and get the matching star."* Continue until all of the felt symbols have been matched with the gameboard symbols.

Now have the children bring the symbols back to the felt board by saying, *"Sol, what symbol is in box number 9? (Answer) Please put it back on the felt board."* Continue until you have all of the symbols back.

Dreidel fun

Hay

Gimmel

Shin

Nun

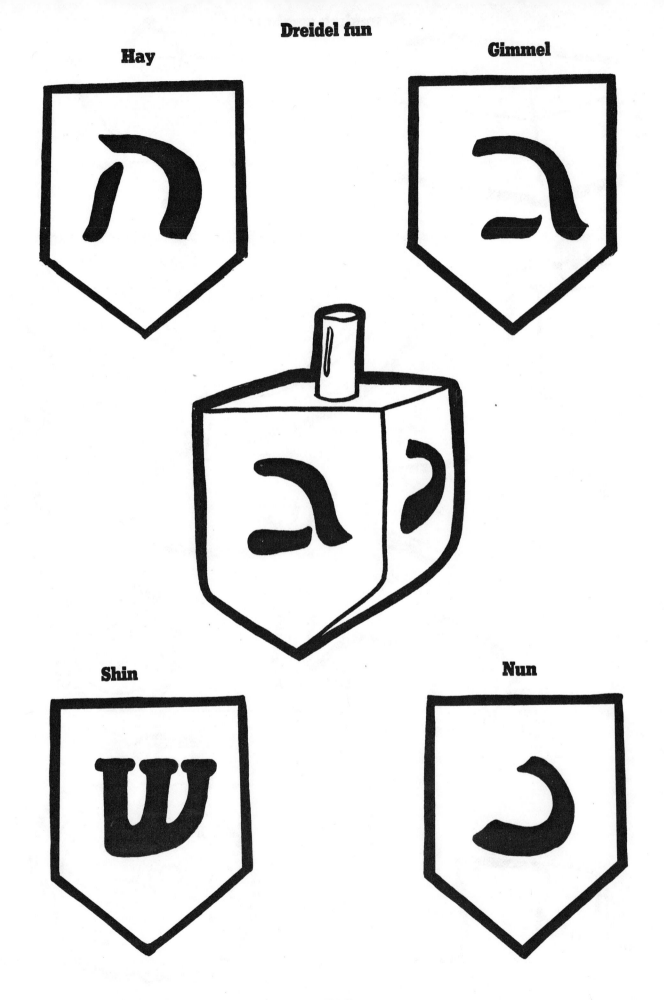

210

Make

A large, medium, small, and very tiny gift wrapped box
Several odd shaped gift boxes

Props

Large sheet of paper and marker

Holiday gifts: Put all of the felt gift boxes on the board. Enjoy a conversation with the children about gifts they have received. See if any of them can remember different items they were given which came in small, very tiny and large boxes.

When you have finished talking about gifts they have received, point to one of the felt packages on the board. First decide what size gift would fit into the box you are pointing at. Then have the children think of all the items that might be in the box. Write down all of their ideas on a large sheet of paper. As you discuss the possibilities, also think of which family member might like it. When they have thought of every possibility, take the gift box off of the board and tape it next to the list they developed. Continue with another package.

Make

A large stocking

Fill the stocking: Put an empty stocking on the board. Say to the children, *"Santa is looking through his pack for several small gifts a child would like. Now if you were Santa, what presents would you take out of your big pack and put into this child's stocking?"* Encourage the children to think of small gifts that would fit into the stocking. (If your children are beginning to read, make a list of the presents they mention. Hang the list for everyone to read.)

Make

Matching sets of candy canes with different colored patterns

Candy canes: Candy canes are one of the most popular sweets of the holiday season. Put one set of candy canes on the felt board. Pass the other set out to the children. Point to one of the candy canes on the felt board. Have the children look at it and 'read' the order of the stripes — for example, *"red, yellow, white; red, yellow, white"*. Now have them look at their candy cane. If they have one that is the same pattern as the one on the board, they should put it on the board near the original one.

Make

A large Christmas tree
Several colored lights
Ornaments
   Teddy bear
   Candy cane
   Angel
   Drum
   Stocking
   Sailboat
   Star
   Snowman
   Stable
   Ball
   Bell
   And others

Props

Short pieces of black yarn

Decorate the tree: Put the large felt tree on the board. Now begin to decorate. First come the colored lights. Slowly put each light on the tree and have the children call out the color of the light. Then connect the lights with the yarn. Say, *"Joel, come up and connect the red and yellow lights."* Continue until all of the lights are connected.

Next hang the ornaments. Pass them out so each child gets at least one to hang on the tree. When each child has an ornament, say a riddle describing a certain one, such as, *"If you have a red and white striped ornament, come and place it where you wish on the tree."* Proceed until the entire tree is decorated. Then put the last one on top.

Enjoy talking about your tree and other ones the children have decorated.

Fill the stocking

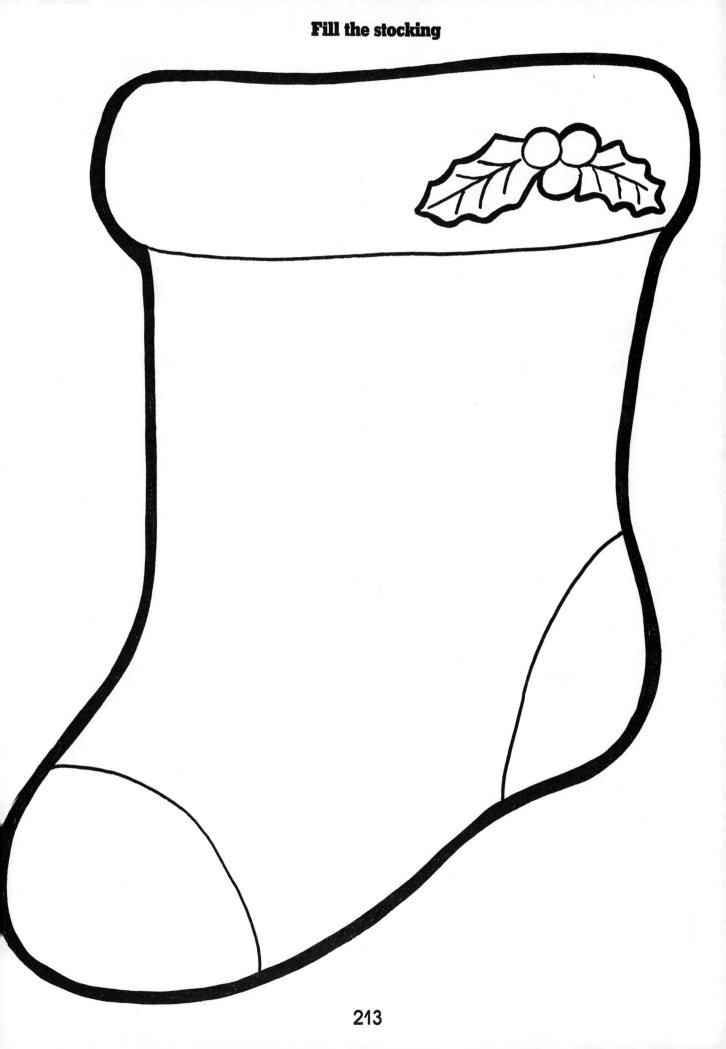

Candy canes

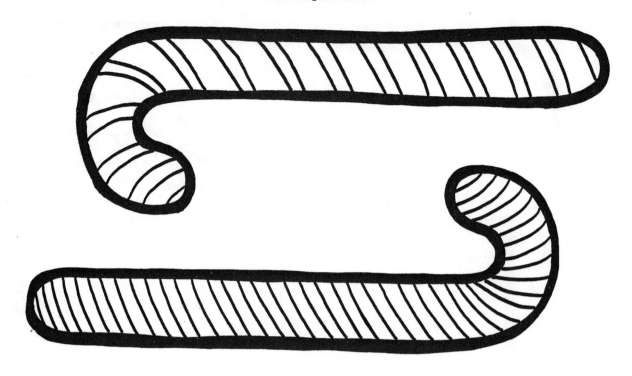

Decorate the tree

Tree Top

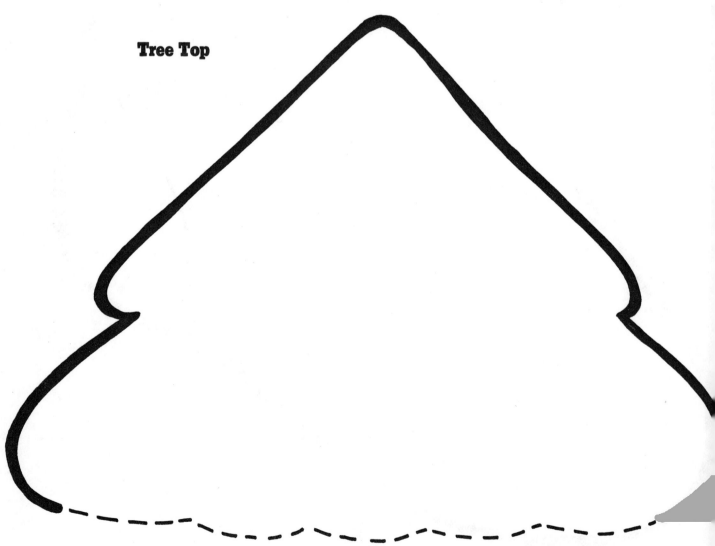

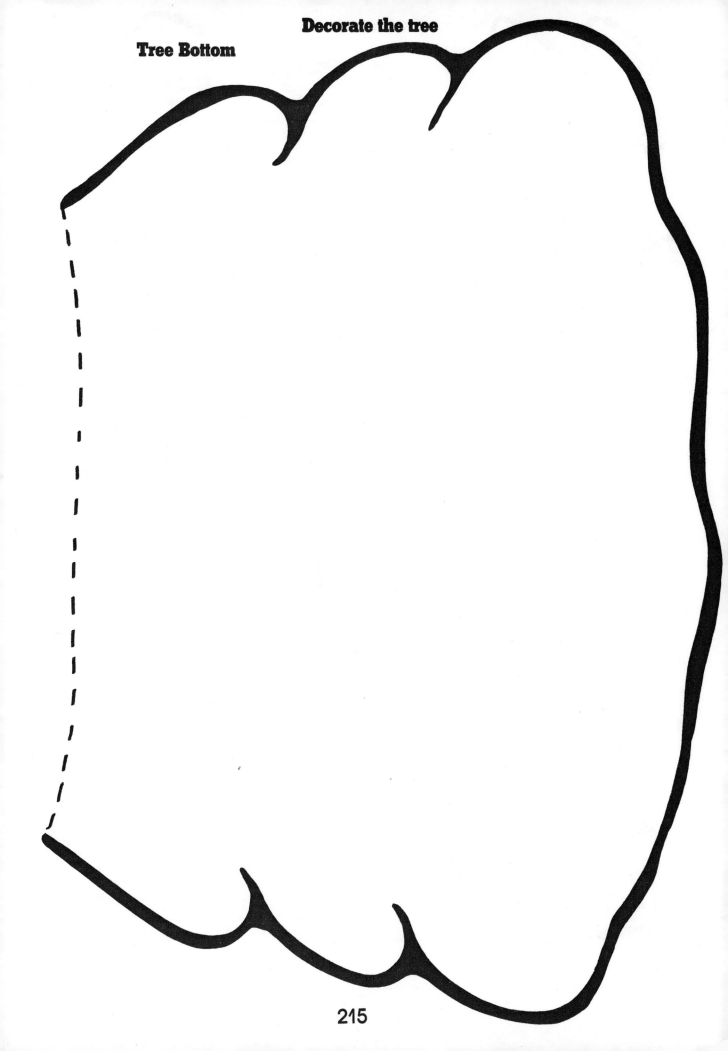

Tree Bottom

Decorate the tree

215

Decorate the tree

Index

FOR EVERY MONTH

BUILDING BLOCKS

an activity newspaper for adults
and their young children

**TAKE
A LOOK
AT
BUILDING
BLOCKS
NEWSPAPER**

PUBLISHED:
10 times a year
including an expanded
summer issue.

RATES:
1 Year ~ $20⁰⁰
2 Years ~ $36⁵⁰
3 Years ~ $50⁰⁰
Sample ~ $ 3⁰⁰

SEND YOUR NAME, ADDRESS
(INCLUDING ZIP CODE), AND
PAYMENT TO:

BUILDING BLOCKS
38W567 Brindlewood
Elgin, Il 60123

BUILDING BLOCKS is a 20 page early
childhood activity newspaper offering a total
curriculum resource to use in your classroom
and share with your parents.

MONTHLY FEATURES include:

~ Reproducible parent activity calendar.

~ Activity pages highlighting language, art,
physical, science/math, creative, and self/social
activities which are easy to plan and
implement.

~ Ready-to-use charts, games, and/or posters.

~ Special activity page for toddlers and twos.

~ Large easy-to-use illustrations.

~ 4 page **FEATURED TOPIC** *Pull-Out Section*.

BUILDING BLOCKS

Felt Board Fun

by Liz and Dick Wilmes. Make your felt board come alive. Discover how versatile it is as the children become involved with a wide range of activities. This unique book has over 150 ideas with accompanying patterns.
ISBN 0-943452-02-3 $14.95

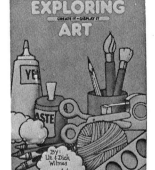

Parachute Play

by Liz and Dick Wilmes. A year 'round approach to one of the most versatile pieces of large muscle equipment. Starting with basic techniques, PARACHUTE PLAY provides over 100 activities to use with your parachute.
ISBN 0-943452-03-1 $7.95

Exploring Art

by Liz and Dick Wilmes. EXPLORING ART is divided by months. Over 250 art ideas for paint, chalk, doughs, etc. plus a display suggestion.
ISBN 0-943452-05-8 $16.95

Everyday Bulletin Boards

by Wilmes and Moehling. Features open-ended bulletin board activities which the children can create plus boards which teachers can make and use to enhance their curriculum. Truly a bulletin board book for the early childhood classroom.
ISBN 0-943452-09-0 $8.95

Gifts, Cards, And Wraps

by Wilmes and Zavodsky. Help the children sparkle with the excitement of gift-giving. Filled with thoughtful gifts, unique wraps, and special cards which the children can easily make and give. They're sure to bring smiles.
ISBN 0-943452-06-6 $7.95

Imagination Stretchers

by Liz and Dick Wilmes. Perfect for whole language. Over 400 conversation starters for creative discussions, simple lists, and beginning dictations and writing.
ISBN 0-943452-04-X $6.95

Parent Programs and Open Houses

by Susan Spaete. Filled with a wide variety of year 'round presentations, pre-registration ideas, open houses, and end-of-the-year gatherings. All involve the children from the planning stages through the programs.
ISBN 0-943452-08-2 $9.95

Classroom Parties

by Susan Spaete. Each party suggests decorations, trimmings, and snacks which the children can easily make to set a festive mood. Choose from games, songs, art activities, stories, and related experiences which will add to the excitement and fun.
ISBN 0-943452-07-4 $8.95

The Circle Time Book

by Liz and Dick Wilmes. THE CIRCLE TIME BOOK captures the spirit of seasons and holidays. It is filled with more than 400 circle time activities, including fingerplays, language activities, active games, and more.
ISBN 0-943452-00-7 $8.95

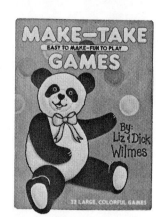

Everyday Circle Times

by Liz and Dick Wilmes. Over 900 ideas for Circle Time! Choose activities from 48 different topics divided into seven sections: self-concept, concepts, animals, foods, science, occupations, and recreation.
ISBN 0-943452-01-5 $12.95

Yearful of Circle Times

by Liz and Dick Wilmes. YEARFUL is the third book in the Circle Time Series! It highlights 52 more topics to use on a weekly/seasonal basis or mixed and matched according to your curriculum. A perfect companion to THE CIRCLE TIME BOOK and EVERYDAY CIRCLE TIMES.
ISBN 0-943452-10-4 $14.95

Learning Centers

by Liz and Dick Wilmes. Hundreds of open-ended activities to quickly involve and excite your children. You'll use it every time you plan and whenever you need a quick, additional activity. A must for every teacher's bookshelf.
ISBN 0-943452-13-9 $14.95

Make-Take Games

by Liz and Dick Wilmes. Features 32 large, colorful games which are easy to make. Children will have fun everyday playing them by themselves or in groups.
ISBN 0-943452-11-2 $12.95

Companion Pattern Set

Game-making made even easier! Set of giant pattern sheets to accompany MAKE-TAKE GAMES. Ready-to-use, a great time saver. Plus use the patterns for so many other activities which need a visual aid.
ISBN 0-943452-12-0 $24.95

FOR YOUR ORDER

NAME: _____

ADDRESS: _____

CITY: _____

STATE: _____ ZIP: _____

AVAILABLE FROM BOOKSTORES
SCHOOL SUPPLY STORES
OR ORDER DIRECTLY FROM:

38W567 Brindlewood, Elgin, Illinois 60123
708-742-1013   800-233-2448   708-742-1054(FAX)

QTY.		EACH	TOTAL
____	BUILDING BLOCKS Subscription	20.00	____
____	CIRCLE TIME BOOK - HOLIDAYS	8.95	____
____	CLASSROOM PARTIES	8.95	____
____	EVERYDAY BULLETIN BOARDS	8.95	____
____	EVERYDAY CIRCLE TIMES	12.95	____
____	EXPLORING ART	16.95	____
____	FELT BOARD FUN	12.95	____
____	GIFTS, CARDS, AND WRAPS	7.95	____
____	IMAGINATION STRETCHERS	6.95	____
____	LEARNING CENTERS	14.95	____
____	MAKE-TAKE GAMES	12.95	____
____	MAKE-TAKE PATTERN SET	24.95	____
____	PARACHUTE PLAY	7.95	____
____	PARENT PROGRAMS/OPEN HOUSES	9.95	____
____	YEARFUL OF CIRCLE TIMES	14.95	____

TOTAL _____